VICTOR MARX

FOREWORD BY CHARLIE KIRK

THE DANGEROUS GENTLEMAN

A CALL FOR MEN TO BE *COURAGEOUS* IN A CULTURE OF FEAR.

Unless otherwise marked, all Scriptures are taken from ESV® Bible (The Holy Bible, English Standard Version®), copyright © 2001 by Crossway, a publishing ministry of Good News Publishers. Used by permission. All rights reserved.

Scriptures marked NIV are taken from the Holy Bible, New International Version®, NIV®. Copyright © 1973, 1978, 1984, 2011 by Biblica, Inc. ® Used by permission of Zondervan. All rights reserved worldwide. www.zondervan.com. The "NIV" and "New International Version" are trademarks registered in the United States Patent and Trademark Office by Biblica, Inc.®

Cataloging-in-Publication data on file with the Library of Congress.

Hardcover ISBN: 979-8-9900632-0-4
Paperback ISBN: 979-8-9900632-1-1

Published in the United States by
Onesimus Publishing
PO Box 88327
Colorado Springs, CO 80908-8327
Manufactured in the United States of America

10 9 8 7 6 5 4 3 2 1

Books are available in quantity for promotional or premium use. For information on discounts and terms, please visit our website: dangerousgentleman.com.

I dedicate this book to my bride, Eileen, who helped me become the Dangerous Gentleman I have wanted to be since I was a child. And to Jesus, who is the best example of a Dangerous Gentleman.

CONTENTS

FOREWORD

In a world often clouded by uncertainty, immorality, and disinformation—a world in which some struggle to define what a woman is or label masculinity as evil—Victor Marx's *The Dangerous Gentleman* is a beacon of clarity, virtue, and inspiration.

This extraordinary book is more than just a collection of incredible, humbling, and life-changing stories. It is a powerful testament to the remarkable journey of a man who embodies a life well-lived in the service of his family, nation, and God.

In these pages, you will embark on a riveting voyage from the most treacherous corners of our world to the tenderest chambers of the human heart. Victor Marx's story unfolds with unapologetic candor and authenticity. His journey from a tumultuous past to a purpose-driven present testifies to the redemptive power of faith, resilience, purpose, and friendship.

I have had the privilege of knowing Victor as a dear friend for many years. It's difficult to describe this incredible man: unyielding determination, boundless humor, unmatched courage, inspiring compassion, and a commitment to humanity's greater good. As you read these chapters—each one a captivating episode in Victor's life—you'll come to realize that "remarkable" simply does not do justice of the life he has led and the impact he's made.

The Dangerous Gentleman not only chronicles Victor's high-risk missions into war-torn regions, his encounters with terror and darkness, and his tireless efforts to bring light to the lives of the vulnerable, but distills profound life lessons from each adventure. Whether it's navigating a jungle, confronting demons, saving the abused, or putting troubled youth on the right path, every story carries a universal message of hope, love, courage, and faith.

This book is also a rallying cry to awaken the "dangerous gentleman" within each of us. It is a call to rise above complacency, to shatter the limitations we place on ourselves, and to embrace the higher purpose of each of our lives. Victor Marx embodies this audacity to live life to the fullest and with purpose.

The Dangerous Gentleman will make you laugh. It will make you hold your breath in suspense. It'll move you to tears. It will challenge your notions of what it means to be both dangerous and gentle in a world that so desperately needs "dangerous gentlemen." It is my sincere belief that the pages you are about to turn will inspire you to discover a new dimension of what's possible within your own life. I know it has for me.

As you embark on this journey with Victor, I encourage you to immerse yourself fully and let the stories seep into your soul. And as you turn the pages, remember that you, too, have the potential to be a dangerous gentleman—to be a force for good, a beacon of hope, and a catalyst for change.

I hope that *The Dangerous Gentleman* takes you on a journey to discovering in your own life the meaning of real courage, human compassion, virtuous masculinity, and the unwavering pursuit of a life that ends with our Lord calling to you, "Well done, good and faithful servant."

Charlie Kirk

CHAPTER 1

JUNGLE ATTACK

It was my third night deep in the jungles of Burma, and already I was planning my escape.

No, I wasn't being held hostage by hostile forces, but rather by a commitment I'd made to a new friend, Dave Eubank, founder and leader of the Free Burma Rangers. FBR is what you might call an armed relief group that works in contested territory in Burma and beyond. As I was to find out, it probably would have been easier to escape from hostile forces than from Dave himself.

I was there because God had told me to go and I had obeyed, somewhat to my chagrin. Dave and I, both "high-risk missionaries," as we are often called, had certainly bonded when we'd met a few months earlier in Southern California. Now he wanted me to train the whip-strong soldiers and soldierettes under his leadership in the fine arts of wielding knives and using firearms. The idea was to teach these brave young people how to effectively perform close, hand-to-hand combat with Burmese government troops, if things came to that.

The problem was that I'd gotten really sick upon landing in Burma, before we even started the hike in. I managed to stagger along with the team on a two-day pump from base camp to this interior military-and-relief encampment. Now I felt as weak as a newborn kitten—and I was supposed to start training people in the morning.

Lying there in my hammock in a dark, windowless hut, feeling sick as a stray dog, I had it all planned out. I'd (briefly) seen the work Dave, his wife, and their children were doing alongside their hundreds of well-trained jungle humanitarian-warriors. I could enthusiastically tell people back in the States about their amazing exploits—rescuing and supporting innocent war victims on the muddy, vine-tangled slopes of that strife-torn country.

I'll wake up and tell Dave it's all good, I thought to myself in the dark. *I saw the ministry and now I can go back and help him raise a bunch of money. His soldiers will understand. They probably know how to work a blade and a firearm better than I do, anyway. They don't need me here.*

This exit plan comforted me. In fact, I'd just woken up from a dream about leaving Burma, which I took as heavenly confirmation—and my ticket out of this hut, this country, and this assignment.

It'll be good to get back to Eileen, to the kids, to safe drinking water and decent coffee, I thought.

I smiled in spite of my sickness and rolled the comforting thoughts around in my head. Then I noticed movement near the door of the hut. Dave entered, wearing a softly glowing red headlamp. He crept over to my hammock with the ease and stealth of an elite soldier.

For you to understand what happened next, I need to tell you a little about Dave. Let's say it this way: There are times you love Dave and times you get aggravated by him because of his motivational intensity. Don't get me wrong; Dave is an incredible leader. By that I don't mean he's overly physically imposing or domineering. He's actually rather nondescript—not very tall, not mean-looking, and certainly not angry. He doesn't yell. In fact, if you ran into him at the grocery store you might think he was a P.E. teacher heading home from school. (That's okay, Dave—people think I'm an escaped convict and look for my ankle monitor.) But Dave is as tough as brass knuckles, and he has this way of smiling peacefully while pushing you beyond your maximum perceived output.

That's the part I hate.

Dave knew I'd gone to bed with a fever. He was well aware of my illness and the fact that I wasn't faking it. Now he ninja-ed up next to me and placed a hand on my forehead, as tender as a mother.

"Hey, Victor, how ya doing?" he whispered, when he noticed I was awake.

"I'm okay, Dave," I said. I was literally sweating from the fever. I launched right in: "You know, I've been thinking. My work is done here. I believe I'm supposed to go back and raise a million dollars for what you're doing."

Any amount of money, I thought. *Just book me a ticket.*

I paused for his response, ready at any time to follow up with the dream I'd had of me leaving Burma. Truthfully, I didn't know how Dave would react. He was retired from the US Army and had worked with Special Forces, so I knew it was possible he would say, "Marine, you'd better suck it up and do your duty. I'm not letting you leave, and if you try, I'll send someone to hunt you down and bring you back."

But this gentleman-warrior surprised me. He considered what I said. I watched his face in the red light. After a moment, he replied, "Well, we could use the million dollars, Victor, but it would mean more to the people here if you stayed."

There's such power in the truth. I strongly resented it at that moment.

"Really?" I groaned meekly, still sweating, and now doubting the integrity of the dream I'd just had.

Dave nodded.

"Victor, they know all about you," he said quietly. "It's an honor for them to be trained by you. The fact that you're here will embolden and encourage them to go out, fight the enemy, and save people—not flee and leave people to die."

How incredibly stupid is this? I thought. Because now I knew I had no choice.

"Alright, Dave. I trust you," I said, too weak to argue. "I'll do it, if you think it's best."

He smiled as only Dave can, as if he'd just seen something really nice happen. Then he crept out of the hut, apparently satisfied that I would survive the night.

Somehow, I drifted back to sleep. The next morning arrived with aggressive heat and humidity before I even rolled out of my hammock. I got to my feet, pale and trembling. It took some doing not to fall over.

Okay, I have to get water in me, I thought. *This ain't working yet.*

Piercing light halted me outside. Squinting, I slowly made my way in the direction where water seemed most likely to be found. Behind me was the big dirt training area where the Free Burma Rangers, this incredible volunteer army of humanitarian soldiers, met routinely for calisthenics and exercises. It was anchored by a big rock where the leader stood to direct them. I dared not look back lest someone catch my eye. Step by step, I made my way forward.

Bursting into my peripheral vision came Dave, heedless of my pain.

"Victor, how're you doing this morning?" he asked.

"Great," I lied obviously.

"Good. You're up first," he informed me.

"What?" I said, stopping and teetering a bit.

"You're up first for instruction," he repeated. "It's your class."

"Dave, I need one more day," I pleaded. My new plan was to hydrate, rest, and get a running start at teaching a few classes in a couple of days.

"Our schedule doesn't allow it," Dave said practically. "We're tight."

"Can we at least move it to the afternoon?" I almost begged.

"No," he said lightly but firmly. "This morning. You'll be all right."

He smiled, his head slightly tilted, truly happy to be with me. But I was no longer happy to be with him.

Not only do I not want to do this, but I don't want to get you a million dollars either, I thought. *You are on your own, buddy.*

Some unkind thoughts about the US Army floated through this former Marine's foggy brain, but before I could make a move or say a word, Dave's hand was on my sweaty back, guiding me toward the instruction area. Ahead, in that large clearing, stood 150 young people, warriors all—mostly proven and battle-tested. Standing a little apart, and with a more authoritative bearing, was Dave's cadre of even more highly seasoned warriors.

There is no way out of this, I thought. *I'd have to die before Dave would let me not teach. Even if I did die, I think he'd prop me up and pretend.*

So as we walked, I did what men in unfavorable situations often do, and which I do a lot anyway: I prayed. Hard.

Lord, I'm about to get humbled really bad, and I guess I need it, 'cause I'm here and can't get out of this. I submit my will to You. If You brought me all the way around the world to be humiliated in front of these good people, that's fine with me. You know best. I'll give this my best shot, but I think I see what's coming.

As a matter of fact, I did not see what was coming. Dave told me in a low voice, "Victor, they're going to test you first to make sure you're real. It's how they do it here."

"Dave, no. I've done all the fighting I want for a lifetime," I protested. "I didn't come here to prove myself."

He just smiled and said, "Oh, you'll have fun." With that, we arrived at a spot in front of everyone and stopped.

Is this guy crazy? I wondered.

Suddenly, one of the warriors—I didn't even see him—jumped on me from my blind spot. *Bam!* His body hit mine, full force. Then a second guy did the same thing—*slam!*—and a third leapt on me as well. I grappled and swatted at the three guys who seemed bent on—and fully capable of—pulling me to the ground.

Is this any way to greet your guest instructor? I thought, as they punched me and wrestled me down.

I instinctively pushed at the one tackling and tugging at my legs, fearing he had the leverage to sprawl me out at any moment. He was facing away from me, and in response to my shoving he snapped upright and backward, headbutting my nose—on purpose, mind you. These are brutal, tough guys. I've had my nose broken many times, but this rang my bell.

But it also answered my prayers because this was exactly what my mind and body needed. A switch inside me flipped on and I felt the strength of adrenaline—or pride or whatever it was—surge through me. I yanked the trainer blade out of my belt without thought. Trainer blades are knives made of thick plastic, not steel, but if you get poked or cut by one, you'll know it. It leaves harsh marks.

Shazam.

More guys came at me. They weren't messing around, so neither did I. I whipped the blade across their throats, faces, and torsos, knocking them down and sending them toppling. I spared no force because, hey—they'd come at me strong, and I had to respond more strongly to win. If it had been a real knife they would have been bleeding profusely in multiple places and no longer a threat.

When it was done, I stood there panting loudly, blade in hand and in full fight mode. I looked in all directions for anyone else who might be thinking about rushing me. The "enemy" guys lay where I'd vanquished them—more than ten of them. Then, grimacing and smiling, they got to their feet and nodded to me. I looked over at Dave. The grin on his skinny face practically went off the sides of his cheeks. I could tell he was thinking, *Yeahhh, there he is. That's the guy I brought up here.*

With that, he introduced me to the rest of the warriors, and I could tell they were now listening to me as to someone they could respect. Even better, the attack called forth something in me that changed my physical dynamic and effectively ended the illness. I spent two days doing intensive blade and firearm work with some of the greatest young people on the planet.

And so I survived my first trip to the interior jungles of Burma. More than that, I survived Dave and the Free Burma Rangers.

Believe it or not, when I think of incidents like that, I think of Jesus, the original warrior and dangerous gentleman. I wonder how many days He got up not wanting to minister to people, or fight battles with demons, or verbally spar with crafty religious guys, or teach and correct His own disciples. Jesus was so fed up with people one time that He asked rhetorically, "You unbelieving and perverse generation . . . . How long shall I stay with you? How long shall I put up with you?" (Matthew 17:17 NIV).

I respect that. Jesus didn't enjoy every assignment, either. But He completed them anyway.

He always stepped into His calling and healed someone, or commanded demons to leave a person, or fed hungry crowds. He let compassion lead Him, but Jesus also knew how and when to be dangerous. One day He got up in the morning, gathered some materials and fashioned a weapon—a whip of cords—with His own hands. Then He violently drove merchants and money changers out of His Father's house, wrecking their tables and all the equipment they used to rip off poor, faithful people.

I love that side of Jesus, too. I call it compassion in a different form.

Jesus didn't wake up angry that day. He wasn't having a bad morning. Jesus knew His Father's heart, and He knew when it was time to bring the heat. There's a reason Moses called him a "man of war" (Exodus 15:3). In fact, the most common title for God in all the Bible is "the Lord of Heaven's armies." Think about that. He refers to Himself most of the time not as a Father or Savior or King, but as the Supreme Commander of Heaven's military forces. Amazing.

I think Jesus liked warriors because, at heart, He is one. Consider this: When He sent the Holy Spirit to the very first non-Jewish person, He could have chosen anyone on Earth, but He picked a skilled warrior named Cornelius. Nobody told Cornelius he had to quit the army after getting saved and baptized in the Holy Spirit. Cornelius kept his sword and his assignment, commanding a hundred Roman soldiers. He was a dangerous gentleman full of the Holy Spirit. Just like Jesus.

Of course, Jesus also knew how and when to be a gentleman. He held little children in His arms and prayed for them. He welcomed society's outcasts and scoundrels, and was almost shockingly tender and loving toward the repentant. He forgave friends and enemies for doing terrible things to Him—betraying Him, disbelieving Him, taking His life.

Jesus was everything a man should be in all the right proportions. That's exactly who we need to be: Dangerous. Compassionate. Tender. Unwavering. Brave.

If our society is to be saved and restored, it will happen because dangerous gentlemen step into their identity and do what Jesus did. Dangerous people don't allow evil to encroach on their families, schools, and churches. They resist bad people and wicked plans in ways appropriate to each situation. They welcome the repentant but fully resist those bent on doing physical, moral, or financial harm.

Dangerous is not reckless. It is not angry. It is simply dangerous—it will not yield, and it might destroy. God's danger is always directed at evil. It won't compromise or make nice. Its very presence withers darkness. That's why corrupt religious men considered Jesus dangerous, and that's why they killed Him. They knew His ministry would topple their unrighteous religious system in Israel. That's power, and Jesus didn't even have to bring a sword to the fight.

Warriors in Church Parking Lots

A lot of church men's groups do the warrior thing now. They celebrate manhood with campouts in the woods, rafting trips down the rapids, big sanctuary conferences with obstacle courses set up in the church parking lot, barbecue cook-offs, and sports competitions. Some Christian guys get together and smoke cigars on back porches, shoot guns, and cuss a little. That's all fine with me if it gets us closer to the actual warrior spirit God exemplifies. But most men are, at best, metaphorical warriors. They don't go to war; they go to the office. Maybe they go to the gym. Then they go home. Even many soldiers don't go to war anymore. They sit in air-conditioned rooms and push buttons that make things a thousand miles away go "boom."

Today, we see what happens when men become too gentlemanly—even womanly—and not dangerous enough. Society falls into disorder, crime goes sky-high, evil runs rampant, children are preyed upon, women are abused and stripped of dignity, morality is redefined upside-down and backwards. Not only that; but behaving like a man is labeled a crime and a threat to decency and order.

Something's out of whack, big-time. And it's up to dangerous gentlemen to fix it.

When dads and police officers and soldiers are more concerned about paycheck protection than protecting their wives and kids from a full-frontal assault from evil-minded entertainers, schoolteachers, and political leaders, society is in a precarious position. There are no backup defenses coming to save us. Dads—men—are the answer. Without dangerous gentlemen, we will slide into civic and moral lawlessness.

Yes, brave moms often step into the gap and have done more than anyone to keep this country glued together. But it's not their primary role. Their strengths are different and important, but dangerous gentlemen must rise up and do their job as well. Women can't carry it all. It's embarrassing that we men have forced them to try.

Men who refuse to be dangerous aren't gentle, they're cowards. Cowardice is not gentle; it's passive violence. Cowardice—which includes passivity in the face of evil—is danger in the wrong direction. Cowards leave innocent people in the path of evil. The most dangerously bad people in the world are nice-looking folks, men and women, who allow evil to advance and put up no fight. You find them in bureaucracies, workplaces, churches, schools— everywhere. They sometimes make it appear they are putting up a fight, but in the end, they give way, with plenty of excuses and explanations. These people may seem conciliatory, moderate, reasonable, and peaceful, but they are actually warmongers in different costumes. They are enablers of wickedness. At least evil people might be straightforward with you about their motives. Cowards layer deception on top of it. They're not just afraid of fighting, they're afraid people will know they're afraid of fighting.

Jesus said the first people thrown into the lake of fire will be cowards— those who allow evil to have free rein in societies and families. I wouldn't mind being there to watch them get tossed. Cowards are not worthy of the Kingdom.

The bottom line is, you don't get to be dangerous unless you're a gentleman, and you aren't a gentleman unless you're dangerous. Dangerous gentlemen are full of love and compassion toward the vulnerable, the weak, and the repentant. They are not afraid to manifest each aspect of manhood in each moment under the guidance of the Holy Spirit. You may have noticed that when men are dangerous, society is more polite and orderly. People behave more respectfully toward friends and strangers. They know if they harm someone, they're likely to get their butts whipped. It's like those surveillance videos of ex-Marines or old guys beating down (or shooting) a robber as he stumbles over himself to flee the scene. That's good stuff. That's dangerous men at work, protecting innocent lives.

Our country had warriors not long ago, when we were engaged in large-scale wars. I have noticed that combat does something to the character of a man. It does the same thing to the character of a nation and a generation. It makes us value and defend peace with great passion. It inspires us to protect the weakest and needy among us. We haven't fought many wars recently, but war has come home as civil society implodes morally, financially, socially. Our culture, our families, our churches are in danger of ultimate collapse and corruption. Are we dangerous enough to restore righteousness again?

If so, it starts right where you and I live.

People all around us need to be rescued for all sorts of reasons. How many boys and men around you are dominated by internet porn, unexplained anger and frustration, lack of vision and purpose, fatherlessness?

How many girls in your circle of friends are desperately fighting thoughts that could lead to suicide? How many are silently making radical choices about their identity, or falling into traps like eating disorders and self-harm? How many simply don't feel acknowledged or loved?

We live in a world where people walk around silently begging someone, even strangers, to express concern and help them carry a burden. I submit that there's someone in your life who needs your help to be rescued today. I'm not saying to rush in by yourself and hero it up without prayer, forethought, and partnership. I am saying keep your eyes open for people suffering in silent, dangerous situations. Take a team approach to pulling kids, family members, and fellow adults out of darkness and the desperate traps they are in. We need everyday warriors who recognize threats and respond to them bravely.

There is no other option. Politicians aren't going to save people. Neither are the police or public schools. When all else fails, we must go back to first principles: families led by fathers and a generation of dangerous gentlemen.

This could mean calling a buddy and asking how things are going with his family and marriage. I'm not saying to pry, but express interest and give a clear open door for him to talk. Then listen and walk through stuff with him, giving the best biblical counsel you can.

Pry if you need to. Some guys need that, too.

Maybe you and other men organize a group of boys to go to the shooting range and have a Bible study. Maybe you encourage your kids' friends by listening when they're around and inviting them to church or a Christian group you belong to. Open the door to deeper conversations when you sense the need and the circumstance is appropriate. I'm into righteous boundaries, but I'm also into not being afraid to operate boldly within good boundaries. If fear is keeping you from helping and rescuing people who are in danger near you, you've lost the battle without even showing up. God will hold you accountable for it. What we need now are more relational risks, not fewer, and in most cases, people will thank you for caring enough to open the door for authentic relationship and help.

Opportunities to change the world are all around you. Sign up with God and watch doors open for you to act. You may not find yourself fighting off attackers with a hard plastic blade in the jungles of Burma on your worst day, but God will give you adventures and a cause that are perfect for you. Guess what? You will rise to the occasion and impress yourself and everyone around you, because that's how God does it. He exalts the brave. He's proud of us when we take risks.

When men step into our role as compassionate warriors, we become unstoppable. It's the only way to live—and it's what the people around us desperately need.

CHAPTER 2

FROM THE
JAWS OF LIONS

It was after midnight in Mosul, Iraq, in 2017. The fighting that day had been intense—and so had the fighting in the preceding weeks and months. My team and I were operating deep inside the old city with Dave Eubank and some of his Free Burma Rangers, and a man named General Mustafa, head of the Ninth Armored Brigade for Iraqi forces, with whom we worked informally. It was our last day, and we were prepping to leave. There was a lot to do and a lot to think about.

The night wasn't exactly cool, but several of us were enjoying the relative peace of the courtyard at our forward operating base (FOB), a three-story house we'd converted for the purpose. It was your usual Iraqi fixer-upper: windows blown out, no electricity, no swimming pool, no free breakfast, not a lot of amenities. But a nice wall provided reasonable protection from any ambitious ISIS guys who wanted a quick trip to the afterlife via a suicide attack.

Whenever you're in a combat zone, you never really sleep or rest deeply. Your mind stays on some level of alert. The sounds of mortars and explosions and the smells of burning things—oil, rubber, houses, and worse—are never far away.

I strolled around, decompressing from our humanitarian operations that day. Then something—or, rather, someone—caught my attention. A guy was sitting on the ground with his hands tied behind his back, looking most unhappy to be there. He wore white shorts and a white T-shirt, and had the full ISIS beard and shaved mustache that their sect of extremism requires. Most ISIS combatants fought till they died, so it was unusual to see that our guys had captured a prisoner.

Must be a low-level fighter, some unfortunate jihadist they nabbed, I thought.

But the soldiers and guards around him were taking a strong interest in this guy, particularly with their fists and open hands to his face. That got my attention. I walked over to General Mustafa, the flinty, much-feared man in charge of everything happening in that area.

"Who is that guy?" I asked.

"An ISIS commander," Mustafa said with muted but evident satisfaction.

The news surprised me.

"No kidding?" I asked, and looked at the guy again. Mustafa nodded to indicate it was true.

"He has been captured before, but he escaped," he said, and implicit in his tone was the fact that the man would not escape this time.

As an ISIS commander, the man was responsible for hundreds and maybe thousands of deaths. I learned later that he had planned and strategized major attacks on Iraqi and US forces. Now, somehow, he'd been caught alive—a rarity in that war.

Something occurred to me and, as usual, I asked it before giving myself a chance to fully think it through—or chicken out.

"Can I speak to him for a little bit?" I asked.

Mustafa thought for a moment with his usual stoic, cold look on his face. By this time, I'd been shot at, mortared, and specifically targeted by ISIS, and I had done my share of returning fire. They knew who I was and hated me. The way I saw it was, if you chose to make war on innocent people, killing men and raping and enslaving women and girls, then you gave up your right to longevity and a peaceful life—especially if you voluntarily came to a battlefield and started shooting at me while I was bringing aid and comfort to your victims. I didn't think twice about using my gun to hurt people's feelings in those kinds of situations.

But even in the midst of war, my prayer was always, "Lord, I just want to pray for ISIS guys and lead them to You. Would You give me a chance to do that? That would be the highest, coolest thing."

God had never given me that opportunity, but now it sat right in front of me—if Mustafa would allow it.

The man I admired so much nodded slowly. "Sure, Victor. For you, anything," he said.

Grinning at the opportunity, I wasted no time walking over to the ISIS commander. My Belgian Malinois, Scout—probably the deadliest mammal at the compound—trotted along beside me. With us were Mo, my interpreter, and Hassan, my personal Iraqi bodyguard and dear friend. Both men were highly experienced and respected by the CIA, FBI, and Delta Force, with whom they had worked extensively. I was honored to have them on our team.

It's not often you see a man you know is about to die. Already, Iraqi army guys were smacking the ISIS commander around like a cheap mannequin. Others gawked and grinned at him knowingly. When I approached, he looked up at me as if expecting another punch to the face. Instead, I put Scout right next to him for a moment, just to set the parameters of our interaction. She was breathing on his neck like, "I will rip your face off of your skull if you make a move toward anyone." She had that happy, deadly look.

Having Scout there did a few things. It secured the scene so the Iraqi guys could fade back without fear that the ISIS commander might try something on me. It also had a psychological effect. A lot of Muslims don't like dogs, and nobody likes violent dogs who are right up in their grill. Scout was a destabilizing factor which might help me break through to this guy in the conversation I wanted to have.

I sat down in front of him and looked in his face. At first, he avoided my gaze. Most people assume terrorists are inhuman monsters, but I've met my share and found they're guys with families, beliefs, and life goals like anyone else. It's a strange thing to realize, when coming face-to-face with a deadly enemy, that you're both human. Still, this guy was in no mood to get to know anyone, and when he saw I was an American, hatred spilled out of his eyes toward me.

"Why do you hate me?" I asked him through Mo.

It wasn't much of an icebreaker. The guy stayed silent. Scout panted loudly next to his face. I couldn't help thinking, *This guy was leading the unit that's been shooting at me, mortaring our team, and dropping rounds on us.* But my goal now wasn't to do harm or get even. It was something far greater.

"Have you ever met an American?" I asked.

"No," he replied.

"Have you ever met a Christian?"

"No."

"Then why do you hate me?"

"Why do you say I hate you? I just met you," he said with predictable irritation. Now we were getting somewhere.

"Do you have a family?" I asked.

"Yes."

"How many children?"

"Four. All girls."

Scout panted loudly. I nodded and listened.

"I am a family man, too," I said. "I have five children: three girls and two sons."

I let that sink in for a moment, maybe to soften the ground. Then I continued, "Can I ask you some questions?"

"I'm not ISIS," he retorted.

I rolled my eyes and prayed, *Lord, just warm this guy's heart and give me the words.*

"Regardless of what you are, you're apparently not going to live very much longer," I said evenly. "Are you sad if your wife becomes a widow and your children are orphans?"

Over there, kids are considered orphans if they don't have a dad. Women seldom get remarried and it's hard for them to get work, so they are essentially widows for the rest of their lives.

"*Inshallah,*" the man replied. Whatever God wants.

I looked at him a little closer and saw he was pretty torn up from the beating and the battle.

"You thirsty?" I asked.

"Yes," he said.

I got a bottle of water and uncapped it. Holding it over his head, I poured it carefully into his waiting mouth. He swallowed it eagerly. The moment hit me with force, and the scripture about giving your enemies a drink of water flashed through my mind. How rare it was to actually do it.

I've seen the evil things these guys do to women and children, I thought. *Yet here I am taking care of his personal need at probably his worst moment.*

Hatred for ISIS surged within my heart, a familiar feeling. But along with it welled up compassion for a man in the last moments of life, heading toward an eternity where, I believed, he would be shocked to realize he was separated from a loving God forever. Greater than my hatred was my strong desire that he become a brother in Christ while he still had the chance.

Lord, pour Your grace through me for this man, I prayed. *Please speak to him as only You can.*

The guy swallowed another mouthful of water. I poured more. Gunfire rat-a-tatted in the distance. Voices were audible from the casualty collection point down the street, an old garage turned into a little mobile hospital and morgue. Lying there were ones who'd been caught in gunfire that day—innocent kids and soldiers alike. ISIS was using chemical warfare a lot then, and guys came in regularly with lungs burning from the gas. The man drinking water from my bottle was behind all that and more. But he also had a soul, and he was thirsty.

"Why did you join?" I asked him when he was done.

"My brother left first, then my friends," he said. "There was pressure to fight."

"You became very good," I said.

He nodded or shrugged. It was hard to tell which.

"What would you want me to tell other young men who are thinking about joining ISIS?" I asked.

He got very quiet and thoughtful, seemingly aware that this might be his last opportunity to share whatever wisdom he'd gained in his life. Then he looked at me and said, "Tell them: Do not come to the darkness."

Wow, I thought. *That's about as real as it gets.*

I took the opening and asked a deeper question.

"What happens to you next? Because you're gonna die," I informed him. Our conversation was only delaying the inevitable. The Iraqi Army guys had been ready to shoot him in the head before I came up.

"*Inshallah,*" he repeated.

"I know you care for your family," I said. "I can see it. Do you mind if I pray for them?"

"Yes, please," he said to my surprise.

"Okay," I said, again wasting no time. I prayed for his family—that God would bless them and keep them safe. That his girls would grow up to be great people, great mothers in a peaceful society. That his wife would live to see many days and would know joy.

I finished. He seemed so open that I got a little bolder with him.

"Can I pray for you?" I asked.

He looked at me a moment, then said, "Yes, why not?"

"Do you mind if I share with you what I believe is going to happen to me when I die?" I asked.

"Sure."

"I believe I have what is called the assurance of salvation through the person of Jesus Christ," I said. "You know Him as a prophet. I know Him as the prophet and the Son of God."

Then I shared the simple Gospel: how Jesus had come to redeem men to God. We're all sinners saved only by His grace and His finished work on the cross. I was well aware that for Muslims, the cross is the hitch in the giddy-up when it comes to the Gospel. They don't like knowing that Jesus died. "If He's God, He can't die," I had heard them say. "Gods don't die."

So I tried to explain it to this guy in a way he could handle, and he seemed to kind of get it. I wasn't sure, but I asked anyway, "Would you like me to pray for you so you can have assurance of salvation like me?"

"Yes, please," he replied.

I immediately catapulted into the sinner's prayer and had him repeat it after my interpreter.

I cannot believe this is happening, I thought. *It's like a dream come true. I am leading an ISIS commander to Christ before he dies—and, furthermore, I'm not dead myself.*

"God, I am a sinner," I said.

"God, I am a sinner," he repeated.

"I don't deserve Your forgiveness, but I'm asking You to forgive me."

"I don't deserve Your forgiveness, but I'm asking You to forgive me," he said.

"I know You will because of what Your Son did for me."

"I know You will because of what Your Son did for me."

"I give You my life."

"I give You my life."

"And I thank You."

"And I thank You."

"In Jesus's name."

He stopped. Instead of repeating "In Jesus's name," he began to shake his head "no." Then something strange gripped him. His face became contorted, morphing into a hardened, angular mask within seconds.

Holy corn flakes, I thought. *What is happening here?*

Scout stood up higher, staring at him intently like, *Make a move on anyone and I will do whatever I need to disable and offend you. I am a dog and I get to go to Heaven, period. There is no judgment for pets.*

I and those around me watched as that man transformed in front of our eyes. Muscles bulged out of his forehead. His eyes narrowed. Stranger still, his ears ... *got pointy.* I don't know how else to say it. His ears started sticking out from his head and looking sharp, like a troll's. Somebody else in the courtyard caught photos of the transformation, and it's all there in living color from start to finish. I'd seen this kind of thing in frontline ministry back in the United States, so it was no secret to me what was going on.

But what happened next took all of us by surprise.

With a quick movement and an audible sound, the guy snapped the zip ties *off of his wrists behind his back.* I had never seen that before and haven't since. I couldn't do it myself. He popped off military-grade cuffs like they were threads. He then rolled forward, hands liberated, and started to make a move on us. Unarmed, he was still deadly and knew how to kill people in unconventional ways. Scanning the ground for something to turn into a weapon—a rock, a chunk of concrete, a piece of metal—his mind was operating at warp speed. If he charged me, I knew he would go for the Glock pistol visibly stuffed into the front of my pants. Or he might go hand-to-hand and turn this into a hostage situation—with me as the hostage.

All I knew was this guy had just exercised superhuman strength, and now we were reacting to him.

Scout lunged for him as Hassan pulled out his pistol.

"*Nein! Nein!*" I commanded Scout in German, not wanting this guy to die yet.

From the perimeter, Mustafa's personal bodyguards ran up full speed and tackled him, sending him back to the ground.

I stood there dumbfounded, bewildered, and upset—not my normal vibe. The prayer had me soaring on wings of hope. This terrorist had gone through the steps of salvation with me, almost to the finish line. He was on the verge, it seemed, of becoming a brother in Christ just moments before his near-certain death. Now the situation had turned completely around, and I was stunned, unwilling to let that moment go.

"Put your weapons away!" I kept shouting, not wanting the final opportunity to be gone if someone unloaded on him.

It didn't take long for Mustafa's guys to reestablish control. They put the guy down hard and retied his hands behind his back. Then they rolled him up to a sitting position like before, but they weren't going anywhere now. The clock was ticking for this guy. I looked at his face. His ears, eyes, and forehead looked normal again. Whatever had come over him was gone, and his manner was serene, almost contemplative. I drew close to him before they could stand him up and march him off.

"Okay, here's the deal," I said, close to his face. "There's no way God would bring me from America to a war zone in Iraq to see you captured at midnight, to share the Gospel with you, without you coming to faith in Jesus Christ. So listen. Jesus was on the cross with two criminals on either side, dying. One called out to Him and Jesus saved his soul forever. I'm telling you now, you can call out to Jesus and He will save you. Do you hear me? Call out to Jesus before you die."

That was the end. The guards yanked him up and walked him away. My time was over. So, probably, was his. Scout looked up at me. I felt crestfallen. Hassan turned to me, his pistol still at the ready and aimed at the ground.

"Boss, I'm very sorry," he said sincerely. "I see the evil come on him and he changed, and he break out of his ties. I was going to just shoot him in the face, but I waited because you were saying very nice things to him."

That was Hassan's way of describing what he'd seen, how I was praying for the guy.

"It's okay," I said. I could see in my mind what might have happened: "In Jesus's name"—BAM! Blood on me. Blood on the dog. A body someone had to bury or burn.

"Don't worry about it," I said, but Hassan was not easy on himself. He had been the head of security for the finance minister of Iraq. His brother was killed by a car bomb, and in a country where trust is paramount, he had my trust completely.

"I didn't want to interrupt the nice things you were saying," he repeated, feeling terrible. "I'm sorry for not shooting him in the face."

"It's okay. I'm glad you didn't," I said. "I had more to say to him."

Hassan, Mo, Scout, and I walked toward the building to get ready for the next day, when we would leave the war zone. I didn't hear a gunshot nearby and I didn't know for sure what happened to the ISIS commander; I just hoped that whatever became of him, he'd heeded my words.

Maybe I'll see him again someday.

As we left the next day, I was still reflecting on what had happened in the courtyard, but I felt good overall about our operations in Mosul that trip. We had rescued some kids whose parents were killed while trying to flee ISIS. And we brought diapers, milk, and other supplies to families stuck in combat zones. It had been an intense series of days in a very beleaguered city, but the simple fact that we were allowed to operate there was a minor miracle.

Mustafa and I had developed a quick, rather deep understanding—you could even call it a friendship—over the years. I told him the first time I met him, "I have no agenda. I'm here to help women and children. That's it." I think he believed me because neither of us is gifted politically. Mustafa was not in the military to collect colorful stripes for his shoulders while trying to become the next president of the country. He ignored the ladder-climbing, position-grabbing stuff other generals did. Mustafa was pure warrior, a stone-cold killer. He preferred the battlefield to the boardroom.

His reputation preceded him in battle. His unit had reportedly killed large numbers of ISIS fighters by going directly into villages and cities ISIS had held and fortified for two or three years. That's a daring and deadly thing to do. Imagine being the tip of the spear when attacking a hornet's nest like that. Mustafa didn't even need all the modern aids—perfect satellite imagery, devastating air cover, and reliable communication. He made war the old-fashioned way: throwing his tanks, armored vehicles, and men straight into the fray and smashing anything that carried a weapon. That approach, and his success in doing it, made him legendary. When the government needed ISIS troops killed on the double, they called Mustafa. When ISIS guys went to sleep at night, they checked under their beds for him.

Mustafa and our team hit it off after he tested our resolve, and we came through for him. He did this by throwing a couple of relief missions our way in dangerous parts of town.

"We just took this section," he told me one day, after I'd employed the Dave Eubank strategy of hanging around, being kind, and building credibility through relationship. "We killed this many ISIS, but the people living there have very few fathers. They have been subjugated by ISIS, which malnourished them for the past few years. Help me feed them and give them water."

"You got it," I said to him through Mo.

Our team, which included Americans who gave money to support this sort of craziness, paid to fly in supplies like flour, oil, water, and beans, which we then trucked into the war zone. I'm not sure exactly what Mustafa had expected, but the fact that we went in without flinching, armed with our own military equipment—guns, ammunition, grenades, armored vehicles, and such—delivered the supplies successfully, and got out without losing anyone certainly didn't fail to get his attention.

So he sent us again. And again. After a while, we became like an unofficial relief and humanitarian unit.

That's the kind of operation we were doing hours before I talked with the ISIS commander. We worked a neighborhood that had just been cleared of ISIS fighters, but they had been dug in there for years and were likely still hanging around just out of sight. Slowly, methodically, we rolled into town with a truck piled high with plastic bags containing food and other relief supplies. The other tactical guys on our team and I walked down the street ahead of the truck and all around it, our guns out and senses on full alert.

"Do not come out in the street," we announced through Mo and the other interpreters. "Stay in your homes. When we come to the door, we will hand the food to you."

Okay, Lord, I prayed as we walked along, the truck grinding behind me in low gear. *Remember, I have a wife and kids, along with a strong desire to live.*

Children peeked out of windows as we passed by. Some adults, too. I tried to discern in their gaze if the enemy was still around by spying some hint of uncertainty or warning in their eyes. I saw none.

So far, so good.

Without letting down our guard, guys on our team began pulling bags of food from the truck and walking them to front doors. There, mothers and sometimes fathers were waiting for us, usually with kids crowding around their knees. They looked so thankful, so needy, so hungry.

I'd want someone to do this for my family, I thought as I walked a bag to a home and knocked on the door. I kept a hand near my pistol because ISIS guys could be behind every door, and we knew it. My big gun was on the truck, but a couple of grenades were hanging off my kit should things go sideways. At any moment they could come blasting out of there, or pull us inside, or detonate a suicide bomb.

Not this time. Smiling faces greeted me. I handed the family food. They thanked me in their language, eagerly and repeatedly. I smiled and turned back to the street. On to the next house. God would protect.

The homes in that neighborhood and many others were connected by shared walls all the way down the block. They were made of what appeared to be bare concrete, fashioned like one-story apartments or condominiums. I knocked on the next door and the family opened up and welcomed me in. I stepped into the house to set down the bag of food and looked to my right. There, a hole had been blown in the wall all the way down the row of houses, creating a tunnel through which an ISIS fighter could fire a gun or run from house to house without ever going outside. It was an eerie thing to stare through a dozen or more houses at once. I pulled back to get out of that particular line of fire.

Out in the street, burned vehicles sat charred and useless here and there. I wanted to keep moving so as not to give ISIS a chance to get in place and do some damage. Enemy fighters needed food and water, too, and our truck certainly looked tempting. Time in the zone is precious. The truth was, we had no idea which people on that street were friends or foes, and which ones might have already called the enemy on cell phones to give them our position.

Our intention was to exit the neighborhood on the other side and return to our FOB, but we came to a place where burned cars crowded the street and made progress impossible. A dead end. I groaned.

"Not cool," said one of our American guys, expressing what everyone was thinking.

"Let's head back," I said, turning us around. "Let's hustle."

We all knew this was no time to dawdle. Get in, get out. No one on a battlefield wants to retrace his steps in a volatile area, giving the enemy a second shot. Our senses were even more heightened as we reversed course.

We're in your hands, Lord, I prayed. *Keep us safe.*

We passed houses we had visited just minutes earlier, and what happened next amazed me. Iraqi people who had just received food now came out of their front doors with trays of hot tea and plates of something that looked and tasted like falafel—they had prepared sustenance for us as a way of honoring us and saying thanks. My heart was smitten within me.

These people have nothing, I thought, *but they freely give. We Americans know nothing about hospitality. We have so much to learn.*

Our guys knew what to do. We stopped briefly to drink the tea, smile, and eat just a little of their cooked food so the people could enjoy the rest for themselves. We thanked them profusely and then kept walking. As they watched us and waved, their eyes seemed to ask, "You're Americans. Why are you here? We're scared to walk outside our own homes. What motivates you to come?"

During many of our operations, regular Iraqis had come up to ask, "How come our imams don't come here and help us? Our clerics never show up, but here are American Christians putting themselves in harm's way to serve us. Why?" They shook their heads in wonder.

I saw again that it's not our good intentions, correct worldview, or even our resources that impress anyone. What impresses people is courage, taking a risk for the sake of something just and right, and being willing to lose everything in that effort. Courage attracts people. It can even open them up to the Gospel.

I thought about the United States, where it's so easy to fall into laziness that many guys can't be bothered to step out of their comfort zones to fight the battles taking place within their own communities—battles for their own families, churches, and souls. They're afraid to stand up for morality, afraid to speak out and protect children, afraid to fight for the dignity of women, all for fear of taking hits and maybe losing money, positions, or power.

Without courage, every other virtue fails. In combat situations, courage means being willing to take incoming fire for the sake of innocent people. Our ops guys and I don't consider that a big deal. We're far more impressed by the people managing to raise families and survive in those situations day after day, year after year. Those are the real heroes of Iraq.

Who are the heroes of America? The ones speaking up for righteousness and justice in their workplaces, communities, and churches? Those willing to lose friendships and jobs and reputations for not abandoning the truth when it's unpopular?

Cowardice and courage alike can thrive anywhere—in the war-torn Middle East and in cushy American cities and towns.

Which one best describes you?

CHAPTER 3

FRONTLINE MINISTRY

To be real, I'm not as brave or adventurous as it might seem. I don't wake up looking for difficult things to do. I usually hope my assignments for the day include a good amount of comfort and fulfillment without requiring a great deal of effort or courage. That's my old nature talking, but I haven't been able to fully get rid of that thing yet, even all these years post-Christ.

I never wanted to go to Iraq; never wanted to go to Burma. I never wanted to go into high-risk missions work, and I didn't even want to minister overseas. When it happened, it was one of the biggest surprises of my life—but something I felt strongly that God had created me to do. He has a way of orchestrating our massive life transitions, and in this case, He started with Dave Eubank.

It was 2012. I had never been to the Middle East or much of anywhere else outside the United States. My ministry up to that point had taken place almost entirely in American youth prisons. My wife, Eileen, and I were also working with veterans dealing with post-traumatic stress disorder (PTSD). People were becoming interested in my testimony because a movie about my life had just come out. I happen to hold the world record for the fastest two-handed gun grab, and a YouTube video of that was getting tens of millions of views, which was cool because it helped fund our ministry.

I was living near Temecula, California, at the time and heard one day that Dave Eubank was coming to speak at the nearby Calvary Chapel Murietta. I had read a book about Dave and his family, so I went to church that day really excited to hear his message and maybe even meet him.

As it happened, we bumped into each other in the foyer before the service. But before I could introduce myself, he announced, "You're Victor Marx."

"You're Dave Eubank," I responded … and then it got awkward as we kind of looked at each other. I started to think he was pulling my leg and being sarcastic with me, but then he said, "You're, like, a legend in Burma."

"What?" I said.

"No, you're known there," he assured me.

I was certain he was joking.

"I'm serious," he went on. "I brought your DVD into the jungles of Burma, and we've shown it so many times at night with a player connected to a little solar-powered battery."

"Really?" I was humbled to the ground. I couldn't believe I was hearing this from *Dave Eubank*.

Let me tell you something: The Eubank family are the most incredible high-risk missionaries of the past century. No one ministers at the level of danger or the scale of operations they do. Dave and his wife raised their children as combat missionaries in Burma. Their lives are like something out of an adventure novel, but it's all real. I predict that dozens of books will be written about Dave and his family by the time he's gone, and many movies will be made about them. One day you will tell your grandchildren, "I lived at the same time, on the same planet, as the Eubanks." Your grandkids will "ooh" and "ahh."

The interesting thing is, Dave is almost totally unaggressive. His manner is quiet and gentle—not quiet with turmoil raging inside him like so many frustrated dudes, but quiet with actual peace. He even has the ability to recede into the background of a scene. When people meet Dave, they can't believe it's him. He epitomizes the "gentle" in "gentleman" without much thinking about it. He is the most authentic, brave guy I know—and I know a lot of guys.

Is Dave dangerous? In spades. There is no pullback, no compromise in him. I would soon find myself in crazy situations with him, avoiding death amidst the hail song of bullets and bursting mortars, but even in pitched combat, Dave seems to be at rest, wearing a sincere smile, having fun, and caring for folks.

He is simply unafraid.

One time before I went to Burma, Dave called to say, "We need two things here more than anything else."

"Okay, what are they?" I asked.

"Head lamps and Leatherman tools, but a specific kind," he said.

"What kind? I'll get it done," I promised.

"We need the model that has the mini saw in it," he said.

"Okay. Why that one?" I asked.

"Land mines are everywhere. All our teams are trained to do medical work, and they do more amputations with that tool," Dave said practically. "It's like surgical gold here."

"You have to be kidding," I said.

"No, it's real," he said.

I think I took a hundred Leatherman tools with me on that trip to give away.

My point is this: You don't have to be a hairy, overbearing, loud, controlling guy with all the answers to be dangerous. You get to just be you—the real you, not some made-up version of yourself. (You don't even have to go to the gym, though a little sun wouldn't hurt some of you guys.)

Back in the church foyer that Sunday, I said, "Dave, I read your book and I'm both challenged and encouraged by the life you live."

In typical Dave fashion he replied, "Great! Come to Burma."

"I don't like you *that* much," I said. "That's not going to happen."

But he looked at me like only Dave can and said, "You really need to come. Come train our rangers. It would mean so much."

I'd known him merely minutes, and already he was bugging me. I didn't want to go overseas, especially to a gnarly nation like Burma. I was knee-deep in youth prisons, trying to help military guys who had PTSD. My plate was full.

"The only way I'm going to Burma is if y'all pray me there," I said, "because I can tell you I have zero desire."

He smiled like, "Okay," which left me feeling nervous. As we shook hands and parted, I was going, *Lord, I'll go if You want me to, but* . . .

There was another big reason I didn't want to go: Years earlier, I had blown out a tendon doing some awesome, manly martial arts kicks. The tear was so extreme that no doctor would work on it for two years. The surgeon who finally ended up fixing it said, "The only reason I'm working on you is because I can't hurt you anymore. You're so messed up."

Seven years after that, in Hawaii at a large martial arts school, I hurt the leg again with a spinning hook kick on a bag. I heard a pop and then my leg stopped working. What ran through my head was the doctor's previous warning: "If you ever mess this up, you'll walk with a cane for the rest of your life."

It was true that I had treated my body like a cheap rental car, banging it around in training and sparring with no regard for its limits. As a result, I lost 40 percent of my right hamstring and underwent many surgeries in the United States and Australia. Spiritually, I learned from it, big-time. I heard the Lord say, "Just because you're not doing drugs or partying doesn't mean you can use your body however you want. Even in athletic sports, your body is still the temple of the Holy Spirit. I own it."

I had never thought of it that way. I didn't consider that overtraining could be a sin, but it absolutely can be. The mind and will are far more powerful than what the body can withstand, and my drive to excel had broken parts of me. That was on me. Now I saw that my body was not my own, even for extreme forms of ministry. It is God's temple.

In Dave's Free Burma Rangers, they did crazy forced marches, humping gear up and down mountains on slippery, muddy trails. How on earth would I pull that off, having lost so much strength in my leg? Because the hamstring is the body's decelerator, I couldn't go down hills very well. I lacked muscle control in that area. My leg would fly out of control if I put weight on it. It was embarrassing.

Eileen warned me; not to be discouraging but to keep things real.

"Honey, there are no helicopters. There is no out," she said. "Once you're in, you're in."

"I am perfectly aware of that," I retorted.

Two years had gone by since I'd met Dave, and we had kept in touch intermittently. Dave had done what he said he would do and prayed me to Burma. Over time, God had changed my heart toward the invitation, and I felt I was supposed to join him for a month to help train his people. Now I was trying to convince myself I wouldn't fall apart upon arrival.

"Eileen," I said, speaking confidence into myself, "this could be the chance of a lifetime, to push myself to my physical limits and see what I can still do."

With her agreement and blessing, I ended up flying into Burma and following Dave's FBR teams up and down muddy trails in remote areas. My leg did not fail, but it was one of the hardest things I'd ever done, physically, and I spent most of my time at the back of the line like the Little Engine That Could.

"You win the award for the slowest person of all the people who have ever come to Burma, including old women," Dave said at the end of my visit. It was very humbling.

On that trip I also experienced a form of violent vomiting previously unknown to me. It was so loud that I literally laughed between heaves and thought, "Is anyone recording this? This is impressive." If you can't change your situation, you may as well enjoy some aspect of it.

Did I mention the hairy, size-of-your-hand spiders crawling around my hut at night? I was dumb enough to turn on my flashlight and see half a dozen of them hanging there like it was nothing. The hut was small and had no windows. It was just me and them.

"Shoot them with a rubber band and they explode. No big deal," Dave told me the next day when I mentioned them.

I introduced Dave to blade work that summer. At the time, he was a knockdown, drag-out, choke, wrestle, pummel-and-pound guy. I told him, "You and I are not getting younger. Knuckles don't hold up. You can choke and hold, but if there's more than one guy, you're going to want to use a blade."

A blade is the last option to keep yourself safe. If you're pulling a blade, it means your guns are out of ammo or jammed. But there's no greater sense of security than knowing you've got a blade on you and can cut a guy five or six times before he can do a thing. I showed Dave how to use a small one.

"This changes everything, Victor," he said. He mastered everything I showed him that summer. I was stunned by his proficiency.

But the biggest thing to come out of Burma for me, in addition to my bond with Dave, was this completely unexpected idea of going to Iraq.

An Open Door to the Middle East

"Someone wants me to go to Iraq, Victor," Dave said while I was in Burma.

"Okay," I said, thinking, *That's weird.*

"There's only a few guys I trust with my life, who will do the right thing in the worst conditions, and I think you're one of them," Dave continued. "Would you come with me?"

I was barely surviving the jungle, yet something about the idea rang true.

"I'll pray about it, Dave," I said, and I meant it.

But when I was able to text Eileen about the possibility, she just about reached through the screen and throttled me with both hands.

"What?! You're not even out of Burma!" she wrote, if I remember correctly. "You've been there four weeks. By the way, your kids need a dad."

I dropped that subject quickly, got home, and found I was suffering from some kind of mosquito-borne fever that took me out every afternoon. I dropped a lot of weight but never checked to find out if I was suffering from malaria or Dengue fever or what. I don't like to take unnecessary medicines, so I treated it like an inconvenience, laid down for a while each day, and let it pass.

Two weeks after I got home, Eileen got a call from a Middle Eastern friend.

"We've been asked by the Kurdistan Regional Government to send a team of counselors to help with girls who are killing themselves because they've been held captive and horribly abused by ISIS," the woman said. "When they are rescued and come back to their towns and villages, nobody wants to touch them. I know your ministry deals with traumatized people. These women and kids are very traumatized, and if they don't get real help, they're all going to end up dead."

Eileen brought the idea to me.

"Hey, listen, there's this opportunity to go to Iraq to help traumatized women rescued from ISIS," she said.

Now it was my turn to balk.

"No way," I said. "I just got back from Burma. I'm still sick!"

So instead, Eileen called several large Christian organizations that do humanitarian work and asked if they would be interested in taking the assignment to help those rescued women and girls. We thought someone would jump at the chance—at least (and I hate that I'm saying this) to use it as a fundraising opportunity, which is how a lot of Christian organizational leaders think. To our surprise, each one said no. That was a real eye-opener. Eileen came back to me.

"Ain't nobody biting," she told me.

"Baaabe," I groaned. I hemmed and complained and refused. Finally she said, "Have you prayed about it?"

Shut your face, woman, I thought with mock anger. I hate it when people call me on my stuff. She walked away with that Dave Eubank look on her face, like she knew something I didn't. So I held my end of the bargain and prayed about it.

"Lord, You know the opportunity that's before us—" I said.

Boom. I didn't even finish. He spoke to my heart clearly, "I've invested a lot in you." His words touched my soul like a hot iron. Tears came to my eyes.

"I'm sorry, Lord. I'll go," I said.

What that meant, I had hardly any idea.

God's Plan, Not Mine

Going to the Middle East never entered my plans even once before then. In addition to my full plate of ministering to troubled teens and veterans, I was receiving more requests than I could handle to speak at churches and men's conferences—all of them in locations where you didn't need to fear for your life, by the way.

But while Iraq wasn't in my plans, the truth is I never really know what's coming in my life. I'm not a big-vision person. I don't make five-year goals, let alone life goals. I don't make forecasts and try to hit ministry targets. I just get up each day and say, "Lord, this is the day You have made. I will rejoice and be glad in it. You have ordained things for me to do. I don't have to go looking for them. You'll give me vision and unction for the tasks at hand. I will deny my flesh, pick up my cross, and say yes to whatever You ask of me. What do You have for me today?"

My overall experience in Burma had spoken deeply to me. It felt like a test, a boot camp, a qualification for a different kind of ministry. I had wrestled through the fear of going; I had put my body and mind through some pretty severe tests in that crucible. I had even done things I didn't think I was capable of doing physically—and I felt like the ministry results were worth it. While I couldn't see what was ahead, going to Iraq—just once—to minister to traumatized women and children seemed like the next step in God's direction for us.

At the time, Kurdistan and northern Iraq were among the most dangerous places on earth. ISIS had, in a very short amount of time, become the biggest threat to peace in the Middle East and maybe in the world. The terrorists had overtaken Al Qaeda as the leading movement of young, radical jihadists, mainly because it was far more extreme than Al Qaeda. ISIS leaders were also younger and savvier about using the internet to broadcast their atrocities and attract young men (and women) from around the world to join their cause. In addition to being tenacious fighters, ISIS guys were master propagandists.

The rest of the world was just figuring out how to deal with this crazy new threat, and the Kurdistan Regional Government (KRG) was overwhelmed. They were seeking help from anyone, anywhere, but most people were scared to go where ISIS operated. If they caught you, you could end up on one of their public beheading videos. But if God was calling us there, He would keep us safe, so we said yes to the opportunity to give post-trauma counseling to a group of twenty or thirty girls and women who had been held captive by ISIS.

These were not Muslims but Yazidis, sometimes called the gypsies of that region. Yazidis serve a god who is a cross between a peacock and Satan, who they believe is the brother of Jesus. Clearly, they have little in common with Muslims apart from living in the same geographic area. They took the brunt of the kidnappings and sex slavery. ISIS calculated that they were the least-cared-about people in Iraq. Few Muslims would endanger themselves to rescue Yazidis.

This particular group of women was living in an internally displaced persons (IDP) camp in Kurdistan. Our goal was to befriend, counsel, and comfort them, and also train local mental health professionals to help traumatized people. Believe it or not, some mental health workers didn't know what PTSD was, and we wanted to introduce them to the concept and the protocols of care. I had become an instructor in this specific area due to my work with veterans, not to mention my own childhood experiences (which I'll share about later).

In going to Iraq, I had two nonnegotiable demands: I wasn't going without Eileen, because I felt she had a part in this assignment; and neither of us was going without a team of security professionals. ISIS was actively hunting and targeting Americans, which was why very few were buying plane tickets to Kurdistan at that time. We would need a well-trained team to guard us at hotels and ministry points and to plan and execute our team's movements the whole time we were there.

Civilians won't understand this next part like veterans and servicepeople will, but we also had to be our own Quick Response Force (QRF). QRF are the guys standing by outside the theater of war to pull you out quickly and safely if things go sideways. Because we were not working with the United States government or military, we had no one to back us up. When I started putting together a team, that was a big deal to some of the guys.

"No QRF? Man," they told me, sometimes shaking their heads. "That's a big ask."

And it was, especially considering I had never put together a paramilitary security team, let alone led one headed into a combat zone. I was working on total faith and asking team members to do the same. I'm not sure *I* would have gone with me had I been on the other side of those phone calls, but nevertheless, I took the first brave step of trying to recruit guys.

I started with a guy I'd met in Burma, a Delta Force legend named Greg, nickname: "Ironhead." Greg is the kind of behind-the-scenes figure who pops up in other people's books but never writes his own. He is what guys in the business call a "pipe-hitter," meaning an operator who does all the hard stuff. You'll hear guys in the ops community ask someone new, "You a pipe-hitter?" It doesn't imply a stupid person. Pipe-hitters, and all the best operators, are super-intelligent because they create solutions. They know how to think quickly in chaotic, life-threatening situations. There are very few dummies on Special Ops teams. Greg is the epitome of a pipe-hitter.

Let me share a quick story about Greg. After leaving Delta, where he'd earned the Silver Star for being wounded in combat, he continued leading Rangers into combat. During the second Gulf War, his Ranger team was assigned to take and hold a certain dam in Iraq. They took it, but then Saddam Hussein's forces tried to take it back, shooting at Greg's team. During that engagement, one of Greg's guys shot an Iraqi at 150 yards—but only winged him, so the guy went down yelling.

"Ahh! Ahh!"

He was rolling around out there between the lines of battle. The firefight was only getting more intense, so nobody was going to rescue him at that point. Meanwhile, Greg's younger guys were getting fatigued, hunkered down on this dam and keeping the enemy at bay. They didn't know how long they would have to wait for reinforcements.

At that point, with gunfire raining all around, Greg grabbed a bag of licorice, stood up, and slowly walked along the dam in full view of the opponents. As he strolled by, he handed a piece of licorice to each man on the ground as bullets whizzed by. He walked the whole length and back and never got hit.

When the sun went down, the injured Iraqi was still alive out there; somehow, he hadn't bled out. Greg alerted his guys and went down from the dam to the enemy soldier, threw him over his shoulder, brought him back up to the top of the dam, and dropped him at the foot of the man who had shot him.

"You should have killed him," Greg said. "Now fix him."

The shooter saved that enemy soldier's life. You might think a consummate pipe-hitter and warrior like Ironhead would have finished the guy off with his gun, but one of the interesting paradoxes of the breed is they often have the biggest, kindest hearts.

After hearing those stories, I told Greg, "That thing with the licorice is priceless—talk about inspiring your men."

His reply was classic Ironhead. He was always downplaying acts of valor attributed to him. "Truth is, I'd had surgery on my knees and had to stretch my legs," he told me. "My knees were hurting squatting down. I just had to walk it off."

Now I called Greg at his home in the Southwest and said, "Ironhead, I want to take you to a great beach where there's plenty of sand. The problem is, there's no water."

He got my meaning right away.

"Victor, I didn't lose anything over there, so I don't need to go back for anything," he said.

"I know there's not a snowball's chance you'd ever go back there for anything, but I'm taking a team, and it's a younger team," I said. "I need you to be head of security. I need you to be the guy."

"You can get whoever you want," he said.

"I need you."

"Why?" he said, clearly perturbed.

"Because I'm taking Eileen and I need one person to get her out if things go sideways."

He was quiet. I could hear him thinking. He knew that if I was talking this way, Eileen had made her decision and wasn't changing her mind.

"Tell me the day we leave. I'll be at your house the night before," he said. *Click.*

Greg showed up the night before we left in an old, junky Bronco he had tricked out with a special engine and a gun safe. By that time, I had recruited a trauma care team and a security team made up of experienced former CIA guys, Marines, Navy SEALs, and Delta guys. I offered each an all-expenses paid vacation to a beach with no ocean, and they took it knowing full well the dangers involved. In all, we made up a group of a dozen or so, heading to a blazing-white hot spot on a one-time humanitarian mission.

Little did I know it would radically change our lives and ministries.

Into the Cauldron

You have to go to strange airports to get to strange places. We flew commercial to Qatar or Abu Dhabi and then into Irbil, with letters of invitation from the KRG. A familiar face was joining us there: Dave Eubank, who I had prayed into Iraq the same way he had prayed me into Burma.

Dave's story of getting from Burma to Iraq was nothing short of miraculous. His only practical way of making it there was to cross the border into China and catch a flight to Kurdistan, but that was easier said than done in a war zone of his own. In the days leading up to the trip, he kept calling me on a sat phone to say, "We're in combat now and surrounded by the enemy. They are in front of us and on the sides. Our only chance is going right through them into China." That's exactly what Dave and some of his rangers did, accomplishing in three days a trip that normally takes nine. I had airline tickets waiting for them, and they hopped on a plane and met us in Irbil.

Once there, we outfitted our team. Our guys had decided in advance which weapons we needed to buy. It's illegal to bring weapons and other military gear like night vision goggles into a foreign country because, if captured, those tools can be used against the government. But you could buy anything in-country there, so we purchased military-grade vehicles, ammunition, guns, and other cool stuff. We sighted in our weapons at someone's ranch.

On the road heading to the IDP camp, it really hit us that we were in an active war zone. ISIS held positions just outside many of the towns we traveled through. Their flags waved eerily from rooftops. Trenches encircled cities to keep ISIS suicide bombers from driving in and detonating their loaded vehicles. The terrain, the culture, and the customs were about as foreign as I could imagine—and yet I felt a sense of calm purpose. Dave felt the same, though he was a jungle guy, and the vast sandy landscapes were not his normal topography. He was asking the Lord what Free Burma Rangers might do in Iraq in the future; my goal was to get in and out with our team and accomplish the mission of giving young women and girls post-trauma care and counseling. Nothing more, nothing less.

All of us felt a little overwhelmed by the millions affected by ISIS and the thousands still reportedly held captive. Local Kurdish leaders told us ISIS made a lot of money selling slaves. When they captured a territory, they converted or killed the men, then sold the women and children to people all over the world to fund their war. We heard sickening stories of wealthy foreigners flying in to pick up child sex slaves and smuggle them out. Many girls were kept by ISIS as prizes to be given to the bravest fighters.

We arrived at the fenced IDP camp where refugees and those rescued from ISIS lived. The camp was like a tent city, home to thousands of people. What's lost on most Western observers is the scope of what happened under ISIS, with millions fleeing their cities, and the fact that they were not Bedouins or nomads, but doctors, lawyers, pharmacists, construction workers, farmers, and all manner of people with homes, cars, schools, and dreams for the future. When this evil descended upon them, they saw their fathers and brothers murdered and decapitated, their sisters and mothers taken captive and subjected to unspeakable acts of horror. Now, in the tents, these refugees slept on roll-out mats and could come and go from the camp as they pleased. Unfortunately, we were told, ISIS operated in the camp surreptitiously as much as it could. The terrorists' wicked influence never seemed far away.

In one of the many tents, we met the group of women and girls to whom we had come to minister. All were in their teens or early twenties. Several others had killed themselves already. One teenage girl had been raped a dozen times in one day, all before lunch. So much damage had been inflicted on her that she couldn't even use the bathroom properly anymore, and she just wanted to die. Others told us how ISIS had poured gasoline on old people and set them on fire. Children were not spared the most wicked violence. It was like the gates of Hell had opened up around them. Of course, like anyone who has seen those things or been held captive and tortured, they all struggled with suicidal thoughts.

Our team's counselors began spending time with them, hearing their stories, and talking with them through interpreters. We had some limited resources to give them. Most of the counselors were women, for obvious reasons, but one member of our team—Chaz, a big Samoan guy who is a prized member of our ministry staff—became especially beloved. Chaz is a gentle giant and the father of six biological children and twenty adopted children. He served as a missionary in the Philippines for twenty-five years. To a Middle Easterner, anyone who has that many kids holds a kind of "prophet status," and because of that and his compassionate father's heart, Chaz was an instant favorite.

So was Eileen, who ministered to the girls with such marvelous grace and love. I had brought her for that reason, and her ability to connect with the women and girls still amazed me. One day she was sitting in a tent with a girl who was maybe eighteen years old. I watched from a little way off and noticed that the girl kept glancing at the watch Eileen was wearing—a special, rather costly gift I had given her. It was white with silver accents, very elegant, and totally out of place in the camp. I wasn't sure why Eileen even brought it.

"You are so beautiful. Why are you here?" the young lady asked through an interpreter. "You are stepping into our suffering and risking your life? Why?"

"We feel God called us here to spend time with you, to hear about what happened to you, and to offer whatever help we can," Eileen said.

Anyone who has spent time with my incredible wife knows that the hand of God is on her, and when she speaks, people listen and feel the touch of the Holy Spirit. Gunfire rattled outside some distance away, and as they spoke, the girl's eyes rested time and again on Eileen's watch.

"Do you like my watch?" Eileen asked.

The young woman nodded in appreciation of its beauty. Eileen held out her wrist so she could take a closer look, and the girl's eyes took in the full beauty. It seemed to awaken life in her.

"Would you like it?" Eileen asked. I almost gasped, remembering how much it cost and how much it meant for me to buy it for Eileen.

"More than anything else," the woman replied, beaming.

Eileen unclasped it, took it off her wrist and held it before her.

"You can have it," she said. "It's my gift to you."

Next time I'm buying you a Timex, I thought in my unsanctified mind.

The girl put it on as if donning a queen's robe. She stared at the piece on her wrist, turning it one way and then another, and somehow, we sensed that this was a step toward life for her.

After a while she looked up and said, "I really know you care about our sisters." She meant Yazidis who were still being held captive.

Eileen simply nodded. After a little more conversation, which now seemed infused with greater hope and joy, Eileen got up to say goodbye. The girl turned and reached under a blanket or in her pocket, pulled out an iPhone, and held it out to Eileen.

"When we were running out of the building where we were held captive, I grabbed this phone," she said. "It belonged to the ISIS guy. Do you want it?"

Everyone on our security team, including me, zeroed in on that thing like it was made of solid gold.

Unreal.

The girl continued, "I only grabbed it because I was running into the desert and thought I might need to call someone. But it's locked."

"Thank you," said Eileen, gracefully receiving the gift.

"Could I get another phone?" the women asked. "I may need one."

"I'm sure we can help with that," Eileen said.

The girl had no idea she had just yielded one of the first ISIS phones ever taken by Americans. It held a potential trove of actionable information that could help Western forces wipe out elements of ISIS leadership. Of course, I was most excited about the ministry our team had done that day, but now I was beyond curious to get the phone open and see what was on it.

We left the IDP camp and one of our guys called ahead to a CIA safe house he knew was in the area.

"We want to bring you a present," he said, grinning.

We took the iPhone to them. They held it, turned it over, and looked at the lock screen.

"How'd you get it?" they asked.

"A girl in an IDP camp took it from an ISIS leader when she fled his house," a member of our team said.

We thought they'd do cartwheels, but instead their response shocked us: "We're not going to take it because of the way it was received."

Our disgust was palpable. "You're kidding," we said.

The CIA guys shook their heads and handed the phone back to us.

"We just can't be sure," they said.

"Then give us the black box to rip information off of it," we said, but they wouldn't. We left with a locked phone potentially packed with vital information—and a much lower opinion of our federal law enforcement agencies.

The Forerunner

Before we left the country, a member of our team called me and Eileen one night at the hotel.

"You remember that girl we heard about on NPR, the one who's buying girls out of sex slavery?" the team member asked. "She's here in our hotel. We saw her in the lobby."

That really interested us because the news report had made an impression on us. This girl, only nineteen years old, was raising money all on her own to buy her "sisters" out of slavery; her younger brother would pick them up after they'd been "purchased" for freedom.

"Tell her we'd like to meet her," I said. We headed down and invited the girl and her brother to our hotel room to find out more about what they did.

They were Kurdish, but not Yazidi, and spoke English well. The girl told us she had facilitated many rescues of girls from their slaveholders, risking her life and her brother's every time. We quickly realized they were working alone, entirely without protection. They barely had any money and didn't practice basic security measures. The girl didn't even know her phone could be tracked, and when we told her it could, she almost hyperventilated. Eileen hugged her and she cried a bit, realizing the vulnerable position she was in. I put her phone in a faraday bag to keep the signal from being tracked.

"You're safe here in the hotel," I assured her. "This is a good region."

She was not afraid to look up and contradict me: "No, it's not," she said.

"These are Kurds," I countered. "There's no explosions or gunfire or anything."

She sat up, took a deep breath, and explained. "The girls we've been rescuing have all been taken to this region, where they've been seen by a doctor who helps facilitate their being sold."

I was so shocked by her words that I felt like the air had been knocked out of me. That has only happened to me a few times.

"You don't know how bad it is," she continued. "Officials are involved. They're supposed to be against ISIS. But they're not."

I saw in an instant that sex slavery was a money-making scheme that transcended ethnic groups and religions. The impact of this revelation left me speechless for a while. Finally, I said, "Here's our number. We will help support you. We will provide protection and whatever you need."

When the girl and her brother left, Eileen and I looked at each other, wordlessly knowing that everything had changed for us. God's voice was in that conversation, and He was telling us He had sent us to Iraq for a lot more than we knew. Somehow, He was inviting us not just to minister to the rescued, but to help do the rescuing. Our goal of surviving this one trip and never coming back had been my plan, but God had a different one. We knew in that moment that Iraq was going to play a bigger part in our lives than we had imagined.

We returned to the United States, and I sent the ISIS phone to another branch of federal law enforcement. They wouldn't take it either.

"Who is Victor Marx?" they said. "No, thanks."

I understood that, to a point. Finally, a close associate of ours took the thing to higher-ups at one of the federal agencies, and they ripped it clean. What they found was a gold mine of information about the inner workings of ISIS, including their personnel, movements, and so on. About a month later, an ISIS leader's wife was captured, which was a major development in that war. No one ever gave us credit, and it's possible our phone was unrelated, but our team was pretty certain we'd played a role in what had happened.

But for us, the future was less about fighting and more about rescuing and comforting the war's victims. So we went from doing safe ministry in the United States to doing life-and-death ministry in one of the most chaotic places on Earth.

CHAPTER 4

SERVING AMERICA'S ORPHANS

I never would have gone to Iraq if I hadn't been trained, heart and soul, in America's youth prisons for fifteen years of my life. Eileen and I, and our kids, served in those obscure, forgotten locations all over America, where the most abused, most dangerous kids are kept behind bars—parentless and, for the most part, hopeless. It was one of the most awesome privileges of our lives.

I'll never forget the day I walked into the office of my then-boss, Dr. James Dobson, at Focus on the Family in Colorado Springs, Colorado, in 2003.

"Doc, I'm resigning," I told him.

Dr. Dobson and I had become very close friends, and I knew my announcement would come as a surprise.

"Victor, what are you going to do?" he asked me in his gentle, fatherly way.

"I'm going to go reach kids who are incarcerated," I said. "There's a whole lot of children locked up in maximum security prisons around the country that people don't even know about."

It was the first time I'd ever seen him at a loss for words. He sat at his desk, pondering what I had said. Though he wanted me to stay, I had a very positive parting from Focus, and I knew the door was always open to return, should the Lord lead that way. But I was convinced that the next phase of my ministry would take place behind bars among juveniles. I could relate to the kids there. We saw in each other the same scars of the soul—only mine had been healed by Jesus. Theirs were festering and needed care that prison guards and counselors could not fully give.

Nunchucks to the Face

My first youth prison ministry engagement was in Colorado Springs a few months before my conversation with Dr. Dobson. I had never spoken to kids in prison before and, for whatever reason, I was seriously nervous. Around seventy-five kids sat on a gymnasium floor at the facility. Security guards stood around the perimeter. The guy who had invited me saw how jittery I was and finally said, "Victor, I know you're nervous. Just do your karate demonstration. That'll get their attention."

One of my karate students was with me, and I had him stand up and put pencils in his hands and in his mouth. I was going to hit them out with my nunchucks and impress the kids. My student stood there, pencils sticking out of his mouth, with clenched fists. I backed up, readied myself and my weapon, then went at him, swung the nunchucks—and completely missed the pencil but whacked the student's chin, splitting it clean open. The cut looked almost surgical. Why he kept standing there with pencils in his mouth and hands, I'll never know except for loyalty, or perhaps pity for me.

"Don't move," I said and swung again. This time I knocked the pencil out of his mouth. The kids roared with approval, but now my student's chin was really bleeding. Someone took him away to bandage it up. I was sick to my stomach about it.

Why did You want me to come here? I asked God angrily. *This is the stupidest thing. I've never hit someone with nunchucks accidentally. Why would I blow it at an evangelistic event You called me to do?*

I moved on from karate demonstrations and shared my life story, how I grew up terribly abused, how I chose to forgive my dad through the power of Christ. When I asked if any of the kids would like to give their lives to Jesus the way I had, fifty-six of them stood up. That was surreal and I didn't believe them, so I had them sit down again.

"I don't know if you understood me," I explained. "Coming to faith in Christ Jesus is like coming out of a gang and you're not going back. This is it. It's a life commitment. Now, who wants to give their life to Jesus?"

Fifty-six kids stood up again—members of opposing gangs, stone-cold enemies, and rock-hearted young men. I took their statements as real, prayed the prayer of salvation with them, and blessed them in their new walk with Christ. Then I called my student back out, his chin sporting a new butterfly bandage, for the final demonstration I had promised: one involving a samurai sword and a watermelon.

The student lay between two chairs, and I rested a watermelon on his belly.

"I'm going to cut this watermelon in half with a samurai sword, without harming this guy," I announced.

You could almost hear the groans. Everybody stared at the bandage on his chin and thought, *He's going to kill him.* I could feel the guards squirming.

Lord, help me, I thought as I brought the samurai sword up above my head. I swung it down sharply, all the way to the bottom rind. The watermelon fell off the student's stomach and hit the ground in two equal halves. My student was unharmed. He got up and bowed. The place went nuts, mostly due to relief.

I then walked over to the warden to ask him the question burning in my mind. "Was that reaction to the message normal?" I said. "Do they always respond like that?"

This tough juvenile prison warden had tears rolling down his face. "Mr. Marx. I am a Christian and I have been asking God to send someone that can reach these kids," he said. "You are that man."

I wasn't quite sure what he meant, but on the drive home, I called Eileen.

"Honey, I can't begin to tell you what just happened," I said, and I didn't mean whacking the guy's chin.

Back home, I was inspired to do some research on youth prisons in America. There were 2,100 facilities and around 200,000 kids locked up on any given night in the United States at that time. I was stunned by the number of incarcerated kids in our country. It weighed on my heart, and I began to take it to God with great conviction in prayer, saying, "God, You have to raise up someone to reach these kids."

I was so sincere. I had seen the impact one meeting could have on them. Then the Lord answered me.

"I have raised someone up. It's you."

That threw me for a loop.

"Whoa. Wait a minute," I said. "I wasn't thinking about me. I was just telling You what You should do, because I saw the need so clearly. Raise up some other guy."

But it was clear from that moment on what my next assignment was. I had only been at Focus for a couple of years, but when the Holy Spirit moves, you have to move with Him. Dr. Dobson sent me on with blessings, and Eileen and I formed All Things Possible Ministries with no guarantee of income or anything. Just like that, we were on our own.

A friend, a businessman in Alabama, called me the moment he found out.

"You're gonna do evangelism, aren't you?" he said.

"Yeah, I am," I said.

"I want in," he said. "My first question is, do you have health insurance for your family?"

"No," I said.

"I'm sending a check for $10,000," he said. "Get health insurance and let this be my first investment into this ministry."

That was so encouraging. His strong support, and the support of others like him, kept us going while we learned how to do God's work in that unique mission field.

Country Roads

Life really changed for us. We bought an RV and began driving around—my family and our dog—from one out-of-the-way spot on the map to the next, ministering in youth prisons across America. Sometimes the wardens let the three kids we had at that time minister with us inside the walls, but most of the time they stayed in the RV or at the hotel with the dog while I went inside and spent time with the locked-up generation, sometimes joined by Eileen.

Youth prisons, we quickly observed, are not happy places. Just because they are for minors doesn't mean they have a summer camp aspect to them. Not in the least. The facilities are real prisons with real guards, control rooms, bars, cells, cameras, handcuffs, and jail suits. You could move the kids out and put adults in without making any modifications. It's for good reason that these facilities are strict. The kids have committed murder, rape, and many other crimes that make them immediate threats to society. Most do it because it has been done to them. Theirs are crimes of emulation and emptiness, not of raw, instinctive evil. Every kid I talked to had a devastating backstory, usually told in a flat monotone and with a shrug, as if he or she only went through what everyone else there did. *No big.* Kids typically end up behind bars when parents, social workers, and judges don't know what else to do with them. I understood these kids by experience.

As a boy, I was as hopeless as I could be. My childhood was ravaged by physical and sexual abuse. At the tender age of five, a neighbor molested me and left me for dead in a commercial cooler. I had multiple stepfathers—one of whom once smothered me with a bag during some military-grade psychological torture as well as abusing me in all kinds of other ways. I attended fourteen schools and lived in seventeen different houses before I graduated from high school.

By then, drugs, fights, and theft defined my lifestyle. I was trying to find my identity. I was an insecure young man who didn't feel like a man at all.

After high school, I began working as a bouncer in a country bar in Corpus Christie, Texas, where my brother lived. I was rather scrawny, with a huge heart and not many skills. When I tried to enforce one of the bar's rules, some cowboy patrons would laugh at me and say, "When are you going to get through puberty?" I didn't seem to be much of a threat, but people appreciated my courage.

The general manager of that bar was a former Marine who had served in Vietnam. Like me, he was thin and not an imposing figure, but I could tell he chewed nails and ate gunpowder for breakfast. We spent many hours talking about the Marine Corps, and he did not paint a rosy picture of it—which only made it more appealing to me. I began to see the Marines as a way to test my manhood.

Around that time, jihadis attacked an American military barracks in Beirut, killing 220 Marines. I walked into a recruiter's office the next day and said, "Sign me up. I want to kill bad guys." The recruiter was thrilled. I became a radio pack operator—the communications guy who carries the big backpack and antenna. I found out I could shoot well, too, so they sent me to marksmanship training school, and I became a competitive shooter in the Corps.

The discipline the Corps brought to my life was priceless. It also showed me I was capable of pushing my body and mind far beyond what I thought I was capable of. I had always been sort of sickly and weak, but the Corps brought out my strengths, physical and mental. I started excelling at everything from radio operations to marksmanship. Then I discovered the martial arts, which became my passion.

In just a few years I felt like I had checked all the boxes of manhood. I could fight anybody. I was fearless and partly crazy. My mind functioned at a much higher level than I thought possible, and I graduated at the top of my class.

But I still couldn't find fulfillment, and I continued drinking, partying, and chasing skirt. Though I tried, that form of "masculinity" was leaving me empty and hurting. That's when God started drawing me, and I was open to spiritual answers. Interestingly, the first time I felt convicted by the Bible was in a college course I was taking while in the Corps. The professor asked,

"Be honest: what are the top ten things in your life?" I knew instantly that my family and martial arts were more important to me than God, and I felt deeply convicted by that. It was like the Holy Spirit impressed the commandment "You shall have no other gods before Me" on my heart. I knew that commandment from my childhood, and I knew I had at least two "gods" before God. I couldn't reverse it without changing the way I thought, which required repentance.

For six months I looked into the Gospel, listening to Greg Laurie, Raul Rees, and other ministers on the radio. Their messages and my study softened my heart. Eventually, I gave my life to the Lord. Becoming a believer in Jesus and serving in the Corps helped me recover and gave me a deep empathy for others. I began to see that the future God had for me was bigger than any hopelessness I had experienced.

After God called me to youth prison ministry, sometimes I drove to those prisons alone. As I traveled down dark country roads, my thoughts were always the same: *Lord, thank You for sending me here. No one likes to come to these places. What a privilege to do this for You.* I meant it. The faces and stories of those kids grabbed my heart. I thought I would be doing youth prison ministry for the rest of my life—and I was all in.

More Than a Demo

But there were plenty of lessons to learn, and some of them came the hard way.

One of our first times ministering together, Eileen was somewhat nervous. We had been to a few facilities already, but this particular one, a maximum-security detention center for girls, was at a new level. The girls filed into the room, and guards were everywhere. The vibe was tense and heightened.

"Honey, let's get their attention by doing a self-defense karate demo," I suggested, knowing how proficient Eileen is at karate. I thought it would put her at ease, so we squared off. My job was to "attack" her while she defended herself effectively against me. But as soon as I came at her, I realized Eileen was treating this as more than a demonstration. She thwacked me with her hands, hitting me multiple times while calling out, "Hyah!" each time.

"Honey, control it!" I tried to whisper, but she did not pull back. It was like the energy of the room got into her, and she went after me.

"Hyah!" *Whack!*

Is this marriage therapy for you? I wanted to ask as she whomped on me. Did I mention she was twelve weeks pregnant at the time?

When she finished, I literally limped to the side to recover, and she started talking to the girls. But it wasn't the tough message I expected.

"I want to tell you today that God sees you," she said. "You have value in His eyes."

Through the pain of my bruises, I thought, *Wrong message, babe. These are gang members, drug users, hard girls, trafficked girls. You've got to say something else to reach them.*

But the next thing I knew, the Spirit of God came into that place in an unusual way. The girls were hushed, some of them weeping. Eileen powerfully shared the message of the Gospel and the love of Christ for them. It was amazing. It made the beating I'd sustained worth it.

When the girls were dismissed, all of them but one left. This girl wouldn't get out of her chair. The guards swarmed her initially, but she wasn't wanting to fight. She was crying.

The warden came over to Eileen and me and said quietly, "She's the meanest girl in the entire prison. Instead of us dragging her out of here, would you mind talking to her, Eileen?"

"Of course," my wife said.

The girl's name was Brittany, and I still tear up when I think of her. She was eighteen years old and five years into her term. That was a long term for a juvenile offender. Usually, the sentences are one or two years. But every time Brittany came up for parole, she punched a guard, kicked a fellow inmate, broke someone's knee or whatever, and they gave her six more months.

"Why don't you want to get out of here?" Eileen asked her.

"I'm too scared to get out," Brittany said.

"Why?" Eileen asked.

"Because I know when my cell door shuts at night, I'm safe," she said.

Her mother was a drug addict and had pimped Brittany out even as a little girl. Brittany met the Lord that day, and we kept in contact with her. Six months later she got out of that facility and went to a halfway house. She wrote us to say, "My life has changed. Thank you."

Teaching Abstinence in Juvenile Prison

Moments like that motivated us in a big way and assured us that God was working. But other moments seemed impossible.

One time, I ministered in an all-male Los Angeles County juvenile facility. L.A. County's was the largest juvenile detention system in the world at the time, processing around forty thousand cases a year. That's a lot of kids to arrest. In this particular facility, violence was so rampant that when they brought the kids into the room for my presentation, a guard stood at the head of every other row of chairs the whole time, watching for gang signs to be flashed and sudden fights to break out.

It was obvious to me—and to the guards—that as a middle-aged white guy, I had to prove I had something relevant to say before the kids would listen to me. If I parachuted in and began talking about Jesus, they would turn on me quickly. My secret weapon was my ability to disarm someone pointing a gun at my head before he even knew it was happening. That's an uncommon skill that commanded a lot of respect in their world. So I went into each facility looking like a nerdy suburban dad and said, "If I can take the pistol out of somebody's hand before he can shoot me, would you listen to me for twenty minutes?"

They would always laugh and jeer and cheer me on. So that's what I did in L.A. County that day.

"Who wants to hold a gun to my head?" I asked. That got their attention.

Usually, the leader of the pack emerged at that point. So a guy came up and I handed him a dummy pistol, which was heavy like a real one and had working parts.

"Point it at my head," I said. He did, and everyone started laughing at me.

"Pull the hammer back and put your finger on the trigger," I said, and he did. Kids were whooping and hollering as if at a prize fight.

"All you have to do is pull the trigger when you see me move," I instructed him. He looked at me like, *Okay, old man.*

He was laughing, and the other kids were laughing. Then, in a blink and with no warning at all, I snatched the gun from him and pointed it back at his face, the hammer still cocked. Meanwhile his index finger pulled in midair where the trigger no longer was. Before his mind could process what had happened, he was staring down the barrel of the gun he had just been holding to my head. I smiled and pulled the magazine out. The place went nuts.

"What?!" the guy said, and cussed loudly.

Now I had their attention. Pack Leader sat back down, and I began sharing some of my life story, but in shortened form because time was limited.

Then, for some reason I didn't understand, I said something that seemed crazy in that venue.

"The best advice I can give y'all on relationships is don't sleep around," I said. "Wait and then get married and be faithful to your wife only. If everybody followed God's commands about sexual intimacy being for a husband and wife, we would have a better world."

They began howling with laughter. Even the guards were laughing, like, "Did he just say that?" Abstinence and fidelity were such foreign concepts to them. One kid, another leader type, raised his hand and the guards let him stand up and speak.

"Yo, man. That's crazy, your philosophy on waiting till marriage," he said. "I've got to share my love with all the girls. I'm a player. Why you think that's the way we should live? Why would our world be better if we did it your way?"

The room went quiet. All the kids looked at me. The guards looked at me. They wanted to hear what I could possibly answer.

Shoot, Lord, that's a good one, I prayed. *Help me! I'm not going to win their minds over with a moral code. I can't just say, "The Bible says." Give me something here.*

In a flash, I knew how the Holy Spirit wanted me to respond.

"Why is God's way the right way?" I said. "One reason is you'd have a dad at home right now."

The kid reacted like I'd hit him in the stomach, cussing loudly and involuntarily.

"I never thought of that," he said, then looked around, so caught off guard he didn't know what else to say. He sat down slowly.

"Your sister never would have gotten raped," I continued. "There would never be unwanted children or diseases getting passed around all the time. Many of you know what it's like when your mom comes home at 3:00 a.m. from the club and brings a dude in, and they go to her room and you can hear them, and all you wanna do as a kid, knowing that ain't right, is go in the kitchen, grab a knife, and stab him in the neck."

By this time, I could see angry, hot tears rolling down some of their cheeks. They knew exactly what I was talking about, and it wrecked them. They were wiping the tears away quickly.

"There would never be child abuse if we did it God's way," I concluded. "A five-year-old kid wouldn't have been abused and left in a commercial cooler for dead. That was me. I was that kid."

The moment was so powerful. I continued to speak and then led those kids in the prayer of salvation. I'm sure there were dozens who meant it. That was how the Holy Spirit led us week after week when we ministered in those places. We saw revivals take place behind bars.

I often told kids, "There are so many leaders in this group. A lot of you just believed the lie that your life can't amount to anything. I'll prove that all of you are gifted in a certain way. Be honest. I'm being real with y'all, so be real with me. How many of you in school liked math?"

Hands crept up.

"How many of you like chemistry?"

More hands.

"English and reading?"

More hands.

"Athletics? Music? History? See? There's something in you that gravitates to what you're good at," I would say. "You should never let anyone take that away."

I made it my goal to leave them with the Gospel message and with words of affirmation and encouragement—the kind I didn't get as a kid. One time when I was a boy, I overheard a relative talk about me and say, "Poor little guy." They didn't know I was listening. I badly needed a positive vision of my future, but the fact that I didn't receive it didn't mean I couldn't give it to the next generation. That's what I tried to do every place we went.

One time I shared my testimony at a small youth prison. A seventeen-year-old guy gave his life to Christ. I found out later he was in for shooting someone with a pistol, and his sister was in the same facility on the girls' side. But something radical happened that I hadn't seen before: The power of God hit this guy when he got saved. He came up to me afterward while everyone was still in the room and said, "Can I say something?" Then he began addressing his peers from the stage.

"God touched me! God touched me through this man. I can feel it!" he shouted. "You all have to give your lives to God. I feel the power of God!"

For a decade and a half, we sowed our lives into the incarcerated youth of America, and God did amazing things.

Models of Manhood

Youth prisons showed me beyond a shadow of doubt that the greatest need in this hour, in prisons or anywhere else, is for fathers who protect, defend, love, and nurture their families and communities. Restore that, and we would change the world. Way too many children are born to single moms, often poor ones. There is no father in the house to provide for them, correct them, inspire them, or motivate them. Some things only a dad can do well. Too often, if a kid is raised only by a woman, he picks up effeminate qualities and gives up on the idea of masculinity. The culture throws all these metrosexual, nonbinary lunatics at them, and kids follow that example. It's sick, sad, and deranged, but it's happening because men aren't standing in their proper place.

Boys in this generation clearly are not getting the dose of dad that they need.

I hear men, even Christian men, make the excuse all the time: "I didn't have a good dad, so I don't know how to be a man. Nobody taught me." The thing is, I was raised by horrible fathers, too. But in spite of all the abuse and neglect and torture I experienced, from a young age I knew I wanted to be a good man. I didn't have that immediate role model so I figured I would find men to pattern myself after. I became an unrepentant beggar, borrower, and thief. Anybody I saw in the movies who acted like a man, I emulated. Anybody I read about in books who demonstrated manhood, I copied. Anyone in real life who impressed me as an honest-to-goodness dude, I took his example and made it my own.

I discovered that in life there is no lack of role models if you're willing to find them. Coaches, uncles, mentors, older brothers, authors, pastors, and friends. Watch what they do, listen to their words, read what they write. Let your desire to be a good man drive you.

The first thing I did as an adult to become the man I wanted to be was join the Marine Corps. I learned to push my physical and mental limits, and learned how strong my mind was. Then I took up martial arts and learned to get hit and choked, and how to fight effectively and fairly. I pushed myself to a level of expertise in that realm, and it also caused me to develop an ethical creed which helped build my character.

I picked up examples of manhood everywhere I went. One time in my early thirties I was walking around Hawaii, where we lived, and I walked past an assisted living center for the elderly. Outside was a man who looked to be in his nineties. I said, "How are you doing, sir?"

"Fine, fine," he said, waving at me.

I had to ask him, "How do you stay healthy?"

"Vitamins and exercise," he said.

We fell into conversation, and I sort of told him how challenging it was to be a dad, a husband, a business owner, and so on. Those pressures were heavy on me at the time. I'll never forget how he looked at me, still smiling, and had the perception to say, "Young man, you'll do fine. You'll make it."

This guy was a stranger to me, but that statement served as a big shot in my arm. I never forgot it, and I have leaned on that encouragement many times through the years. My entire interaction with that old man amounted to just minutes.

That's what I wanted to do for the kids I was speaking to. In a relatively brief time with them, I wanted to leave them something—or Someone, Jesus—to hold onto for the rest of their lives. Many of them did.

Off the Christian Circuit

The other thing youth prison ministry did was keep me off the Christian circuit—and the older I got, the more grateful I was for that.

I think back to the first and only junior high retreat camp I organized when I was brand-new to ministry. Some junior high kids from our church and a few other churches went to a little place in the high desert of California for a weekend of worship, fellowship, and teaching, and I invited a hero of mine, musician Roby Duke, to be our special guest. To be honest, I was shocked Roby agreed to come. He was well-known back then.

One evening while he was tuning his guitar, I sat nearby chatting with him and he said something that stuck with me.

"I'm so tired of the circuit, the machinery of Christianity," he said, as I remember it. "I've done it all, and I don't want to be on the circuit anymore. That's why I'm here at a junior high event in the middle of all these rocks."

I was new in the Lord, not even married yet, and I felt like he had given me something priceless.

"Thank you," I told him. "I won't forget that."

In my heart I decided I didn't want to be on the circuit, either. I believed Roby. He was older than me and had done everything in Christendom that people say you have to do to be "successful" for the Lord—and he rejected it and chose to be with kids at a small, remote place with no upside for his reputation or music sales. He played his heart out on his guitar and his amplifier, as if he was in a stadium before thousands. Everything about his character and ministry impressed me so much.

That's part of why I was so willing to leave what the Christian circuit called a "successful" position at a big, influential organization like Focus on the Family to go where nobody else wanted to be. Not only that, but obeying God's leading qualified me and Eileen for things that God had in store that we could not see. He knew high-risk missions was way out in our future, and we had to show a willingness to go after abandoned and forgotten children in the United States before He entrusted us with the next assignment. We had to put it all on the line and lay down our lives to defend and encourage those kids.

Because of what we witnessed and did in youth detention facilities, nothing in Iraq or elsewhere really surprised us. We had seen most of it in youth prisons—the worst that could be done to kids, the darkest aspects of human behavior, the betrayals they experienced, the destruction of bodies and minds at an early age because of sick, sinister treatment at the hands of others.

Some of what we saw in youth prisons surpassed anything we saw in the war zone in terms of savage, demonic activity. I'm thinking specifically of Christy.

CHAPTER 5

WHEN DEMONS DOMINATE

At a facility in Brownwood, Texas, I was speaking and ministering as I usually did over the course of a couple of days. It had been an uneventful meeting in that particular pod. The thirty girls in attendance were even a bit subdued. I made some introductory comments and jokes, and then we turned to the Bible. Stationed around the room were guards, watching silently.

As I started reading from the Bible, a fifteen-year-old girl started growling. At first it sounded like maybe she was clearing her throat, but the growl intensified and rose in volume.

What is going on? I thought. I glanced at the guards, but none moved. *Strange,* I thought. Guards were paid to be hyperaware and quick to respond. But these guards looked up at the ceiling like, "Who, me? I don't hear anything."

The girl's guttural noise got uglier, like an animal dying or trying to scare someone away. The others were looking around nervously by now.

"Let's sing a song," I said, hoping to redirect or outrun whatever was happening. I started to lead them in a Christian chorus.

That's when the growling girl started clawing her own neck, leaving serious red scratches on her skin. Then she cried out—in a man's voice.

Okay, that was weird, I thought as a chill ran up my spine and all the other girls jumped up and ran for the corners of the room. For all practical purposes, the Bible study was over. I thought I'd seen the deepest darkness in prison ministry already, but this situation was about to show me new levels.

The girl kept clawing herself and calling out in a man's voice. I stood up and looked at the guards. They had actually backed up! Respecting their superior experience with what might happen next, I did the same.

"What's going on?" I asked as I stepped away. "Shouldn't you help her?"

"Hey, man. That ain't our deal," said one guy. "Aren't you the preacher? Because that's evil stuff."

Evil stuff, I thought. *Yeah, thanks for your help.*

"I'm not that good," I said half-jokingly. "I come in, tell stories, and then leave. This is a whole other level."

The girl continued her violent demonstration and repulsive sounds.

"When this happens, she gets strength and we can't control her," another guard said. "She has power."

"What do you usually do?" I asked, still incredulous that nothing was being done to subdue or contain this girl, who might choose to come after any one of us.

"Try to get her into her cell and isolate her," the guard said.

I guess I like a challenge because I blurted out a promise.

"Get her into her cell and I'll talk to her," I said.

The guards nodded to each other and, emboldened by my commitment and probably eager for a long-term solution, moved toward the clawing, squalling young lady.

There are a lot of reasons people avoid youth prison ministry. It's unglamorous.

It doesn't pay well. And occasionally you run into a very demonized person in whom darkness manifests with unexpected power.

More than that, youth prison ministry can hurt your soul and scar your memory. You hear and see things that may haunt you for years after you drive out of the front gates. Furthermore, most people on the outside are content to forget about these kids. They don't have a lot of sympathy for anyone, young people included, who commit heinous crimes. They are happy to let the gears of the American justice system grind along while they chase life, liberty, and the pursuit of happiness on the outside. The truth is, if any one of us experienced the horrors that drove these kids to that kind of criminal madness, we probably would be in there with them.

In our first year, I studied every person and ministry operating in youth prisons, mainly because I didn't want to duplicate what someone else was doing. I'd rather get on board with whatever's working and use my time, talent, and treasures for God's glory, not for building my own thing. But apart from the scattered local, heroic individuals who went into these facilities and established relationships through consistency, compassion, and love for these kids, there wasn't a lot going on in youth prisons. Few organizations made it their focus.

When I experienced how hard it could be, I realized why. Youth prisons are basically large orphanages housing hundreds of thousands of formerly abused and unloved teenagers who've done very bad things. It's hard to get people, even Christians, to care about their plight. In my first year or two of youth prison ministry, my board hired one of the best fundraising consultants around. This guy told me, "You have to change the way you communicate. You can't say you're 'reaching troubled youth' or talk about 'youths in prison.' Instead, you have to say you're reaching hurting kids."

"Hurting kids?" I said.

"Yes, reaching hurting kids," the consultant repeated.

"But these kids are in prison," I replied.

"But people don't want to give to that," he said.

"But these kids are in prison. That's the reality," I said.

This guy went ahead and sent out a letter to supporters in my name and Eileen's with all the classic fundraising techniques: bolded and italicized paragraphs, highlighted words, a stupid little P.S. re-emphasizing the need to "reach hurting kids." As soon as I saw the letter, I called him from my car and fired him on the spot.

"You don't know us anymore," I said. "You're done here. Thank you. Goodbye."

Then I hung up and thought, *Hope I did the right thing.*

I've never regretted it. I didn't want anything fake in my ministry, either inside or outside the prisons. I wasn't there to raise money on kids or make a ministry name for myself. I wasn't there to sugarcoat who we ministered to. The truth is those kids had some of the most tragic life stories I had ever heard. I wasn't going to gloss over that with some audience-tested marketing phrase.

One boy I met, a little guy of thirteen or fourteen, was serving time for raping his younger brother. I looked at him and said, "So, why'd you rape him?"

I'll never forget him looking at me like, *Is that even a question?* Then he responded, "Because my stepdaddy raped me all the time."

One time when I was sharing my testimony and the Gospel message to a roomful of kids, I kept noticing a sixteen-year-old boy in the back who was so stooped over that his back was nearly parallel to the floor. The whole time I spoke, he managed to keep his eyes on me even from his severely hunched position. When I was done, he walked up to me in the company of the guards. I could tell he would have been tall, had he been able to stand upright.

"I just want you to know, your talking has given me hope," he said.

"Thank you, son," I said. "I'm glad to hear that."

I encouraged him with a few more words, and then he walked away. When he was gone, a guard took me aside.

"His dad is in prison for keeping him in a dog cage for years," he explained quietly. "That's why he stands like that. His dad would take him out to sexually abuse him, or have another man sexually abuse him. Then put him back in."

These stories don't leave you. Neither does the hope you see in kids' eyes when they feel loved and honored by someone who comes to visit them. It becomes part of who you are. Your destiny intertwines with theirs.

Another kid rocked back and forth the entire time I was speaking. People usually do that because they're demonized or they have a mental health problem. Rocking continuously is a form of self-soothing. After the message, the kid came up to me.

"Thank you," he said. "For the first time in my life, I realize I can make it in life and my life can have purpose by God redeeming my life, like yours."

"Man, thank you," I said. "That's amazing."

After our brief conversation he walked away and a guard whispered to me, "Look at his pants."

I did and could tell the kid was wearing an adult diaper.

The guard said to me, very softly so as not to be overheard, "His father sexually abused him so much and for so long that he can't hold in his bowels."

Then he said something that hurts my heart to this day, even after being in plenty of these places and hearing plenty of stories: "When that kid goes to use the toilet in his pod, all the other kids—even the toughest gang members—turn their backs to give him privacy and dignity."

He was describing the use of the public toilet in the barracks-style pods those guys lived in as a group. There was no hiding when you used the toilet, and while ridicule was constant in prison, that kid's podmates took such pity on him that they made a rule that nobody was allowed to make jokes about his inability to control his bowels. If someone had, the others would have beaten him senseless.

Even the hardest kids put great value on innocence. Because it's what they all lost—and what they all wish they could get back.

Another boy, fifteen years old, had a tattoo on his arm that said "Lucky." "Why do you feel lucky?" I asked him when he came up to meet me after I had shared my testimony.

"Because my dad will never hurt me or my sister again," he replied.

"Where's your sister?" I asked him.

"She's here, on the other side," he said, motioning in the direction of the female juvenile hall facility on the same grounds.

"Tell me, what's something your dad did to you that really impacted you?" I asked him. Kids don't mind direct questions and usually speak frankly about what they have endured. In this case, I hoped he would remember something good about his father, some trace of positivity to hold onto.

"My dad tied me to a chair when I was eleven and injected me with heroin for the first time," he said. "Sometimes he dragged me out of bed by my heels into the forest in the middle of the night. Then he would yell, 'There's demons everywhere in the trees! They're going to get you!'"

This was one of a thousand times God gave me grace to listen without tearing up, throwing up, or getting visibly angry. Still, my blood was boiling.

"How about when you get out?" I asked calmly. "What about your dad then?"

"Lucky" shrugged. "He's on death row for killing my mom," he replied. "He'll be dead soon."

I had the honor of leading that kid to the Lord, and whenever I saw him after that he was joyful, no longer depressed or emotionless. The Gospel works, even and especially in the hardest of places with the hardest of cases.

It gives kids their innocence back.

Now I was about to test that hypothesis with an apparently demonized girl who was tearing at her own flesh and making otherworldly—or underworldly—noises. The fact that the Bible study had ended seemed to calm her, and the guards were able to walk her to her cell without incident.

Now it was my turn to fulfill my end of the bargain. I was more frightened now than I had been when she was going nuts and speaking like a man.

Lord, what am I supposed to say or do? I thought as the guard led me down one of those long, dismal hallways too common in those places.

We reached her cell. She was sitting near the door on the floor with her legs crisscrossed, her black hair hanging over her orange jump suit. She rocked back and forth. The guard nodded silently to me, then walked to the end of the hallway and stood there. I took a seat opposite the girl on the floor, the barred gate between us.

Lord, I have no idea what to do, I prayed.

"Hey," I said to her, waving my hand. "Hi."

I tend to enter difficult situations stupidly. It's the only way I know how.

She looked up at me, her eyes mostly rolled back into her head, and an unnatural voice came out of her: "I guess you're going to say I'm possessed."

Believe it or not, I could actually smell sulfur and rotten eggs, to the point where I thought I would throw up. I glanced around for a place to vomit—a bathroom, a corner, another hallway. Anything.

Lord, this is unreal, I prayed. *I don't know what to do. Help me.*

I guess the demon recognized that I was flat-footed because it took the initiative.

"I know who you are," it said through this girl. Then it began telling me negative things about my own past. This startled but didn't surprise me. Demons always try to impress and intimidate you into submission, but I've learned that it doesn't matter how powerful they appear or what tactic they take to try to defeat you—Jesus has authority over everything. That's what I told myself as I sat there listening to that one taunt me with true facts about my own life.

Jesus has authority over this situation, I thought. *Even though I don't know what to do, Jesus has the authority right here, right now.*

But the creature had more tricks in mind. As I looked at the girl, she blinked her eyes and for a moment they turned reptilian: There appeared to be scales on her eyelids, and her eyeballs looked like a reptile's. It only happened once, for a second or two, and then the human form of her eyes returned.

That's new, I thought. *He's throwing everything he's got at me.*

I hesitate to talk about this stuff, especially with evangelical Christians, because so many are unfamiliar with deliverance ministry—or are so critical and spiritually proud that they don't believe this kind of thing happens today. Others feel burned by charlatans who have made a show of "delivering" people to enhance their own reputations or pocketbooks (see Acts 8 and 19 for examples of guys trying to do this). But deliverance ministry is real. Anyone who has ever participated in prison ministry can attest that demonic encounters are a fact of life there.

This demon began to boast, "I will destroy you. I will destroy your ministry, your marriage, your finances—and your daughter."

My stomach tightened a bit. I knew instantly which daughter he was talking about.

Wow, I thought. *Okay.*

At that time, one of our girls was in the worst season of rebellion Eileen and I had experienced with any of our children. Now this devil revealed that Hell was specifically targeting her, my own flesh and blood, and threatening that if I tried to liberate this young lady it would declare open season on my family.

Hell must have sent a stupid demon, because that kind of threat just made me mad—and when I'm mad, I fight more effectively. *You're making threats against me, my marriage, and one of my kids?* I thought. *Wrong move, pal.*

Boldness rose up within me and I quit playing defense.

"In the name of Jesus, I command you to tell me your name," I said to the entity controlling the girl.

"I am Satan," the voice replied.

I often have funny, out-of-place thoughts at the most inconvenient times. It's like my mind activates countermeasures. *Danger incoming! Shoot the flares out!*

So I simply asked, "Is that with a capital S or a small s?"

The demon looked at me angrily through the girl's face as if to say, "Not the reaction I wanted."

This has gotta be some demon of insecurity using his boss's name to try to freak me out, I thought. *This thing is going down.*

Now my mind was flying, but instead of being flooded with Bible verses about a Christian's power over darkness, all I could think of were pigs. Jesus cast a bunch of demons into a herd of pigs, and now I thought: *Where do I send this thing? There aren't any pigs around here, but could I use bacon? Does that count? Then I could flush the bacon down the toilet. All I need is pork to cast this demon out!*

Jokes are part of my fighting brain. Staying on offense, I spoke with authority to the demon. "I don't care who you are. You have to come under the authority of Jesus Christ. I don't want to talk to you anymore. I want to talk to the girl. Let her talk."

It's amazing how a person's face changes when a demon gives up control. The girl suddenly "reappeared" and said plainly and normally, "Hi."

"Hi," I said. "Do you know what just happened?"

"I'm pretty sure," she said.

"It's a bad demon," I informed her.

"I know," she said. "I know."

"Okay, I don't care about the demon right now," I said. "Can I just get to know you for a minute?"

"You want to know about me?" she asked, truly surprised. "Nobody's ever interested in me."

"Yeah, I do want to know," I said. "What's your name? How old are you?"

"Christy. I'm fifteen."

"How long you been in here?"

"A year?" she guessed.

"What's your family like?"

"My dad was a satanist and dedicated me to Satan as a baby," she said. "He put me in a circle and offered me up. He and my mom were not together.

She didn't care about me. He would drop me off at her apartment in dirty diapers with lice on me and say, "It's your turn to take care of her.'"

I nodded to tell her to continue.

"We lived in hotels," she said. "I got pregnant at thirteen and had a baby son. His name is Devon. I dedicated him to Satan as well when he was born. I put him in a circle."

"You invited the demons in?" I asked.

She nodded.

"The demon is the only thing that gives me power, and I feel close to him," she said.

It was a stunning statement. Like every kid—and every person—she craved real, meaningful relationship, even if she had to find it in false form with a demonic being.

"Explain that to me," I said.

"He gives me power. I know things about people," she said.

"You do know the demon ultimately will destroy your life," I said.

"Yeah, maybe."

"Do you want this demon out of your life?"

"No," she said.

"Okay. Do you mind if I have people pray for you?"

"No. Go ahead," she said.

"I will," I promised her. "I'm here tomorrow as well. If you're open to it, I can come back and visit you."

She nodded noncommittally, which was good enough for me. I walked out and drove to my hotel. That night, I got hold of friends and ministry supporters and asked them to pray for Christy. The next day I walked back into her section of the prison, accompanied by a guard. A second guard who was assigned to her section looked at me knowingly and said, "She's waiting for you."

"Is it her or it?" I asked, half in jest.

"It's her," she said with a smile.

She led me to her cell, stuck a key in the lock and swung open the door. Christy sat on her side of the bars, cross-legged again, and again I did the same, facing her. The guard stepped back, then walked to her post at the end of the hall.

"I've never slept so good in my whole life," Christy told me.

"Sweetie, it's because we have people praying for you," I told her.

She either deflected or absorbed this; I couldn't tell which.

"I know you because I've seen you before," she said.

"Really? Where?" I asked.

She named another youth prison in Texas where I had ministered, a facility for both boys and girls.

"Do you remember seeing a girl dressed all in black?" she asked me.

"Holy smokes, yes I do," I said, and it was true. I did remember her, with a shudder.

"That was me," she said.

I remembered her because she didn't want to sit anywhere close to where I was speaking, and when I walked by her, she looked like she wanted to rip out my throat with her teeth. Now God had brought me here to speak with her—just the two of us face-to-face, and a guard some distance away.

"I want to tell you what happened that night at the other prison, after you spoke," she continued. "After chapel, I went into my cell, laid in bed, and got mad at Satan. I started yelling at him. 'You made me all these promises! My life is supposed to be great. This guy says God's way is best, but here I am in the mental health hospital. I've been raped more times than I can count.'"

She paused before continuing.

"Then a demon appeared in my cell," she said. "All I could see were his red eyes. He attacked me. Clawed me and bit me. I was bleeding everywhere, kicking and fighting and screaming. The staff finally came in. Blood was on the walls and my bed. They took me to medical."

"Did you tell them what happened?" I asked, not sure what to make of her account.

"Yeah," she said. "They said it was self-inflicted."

"Did it leave a scar?"

"Yes, of course it did."

I felt the Holy Spirit prompt me to ask, "Do you mind if I see it?"

One of the cardinal rules of youth ministry, especially in prisons, is never to look at or call attention to kids' bodies. It is an absolute no-no. But this was an unusual circumstance, and I felt the Lord wanted to go this direction.

"They're on my stomach and back," she said, and raised her shirt modestly, just enough to reveal two things on her belly: stretch marks from pregnancy and claw marks that looked like they'd been made by a three-pronged garden tool.

She could have done it with a fork, I thought as she let her shirt down again.

"Where did he bite you?" I asked.

"Middle of my back."

You can't fake that, I thought. Without being asked, she turned around and lifted her shirt up just enough to reveal what is best described as baboon bites. There were four of them. Each had two big teeth marks and two small teeth marks, like something had gotten hold of her flesh and ripped and twisted it.

There is no way she could have done that herself.

She turned to me with the kind of resignation that passes for peace among those who have not experienced the real thing. It seemed to me she wasn't asking for pity or attention. Rather, her soul was crying out for a new kind of life.

"Is today the day you want to surrender your life to the Lord?" I asked her.

Christy thought quietly for a moment, then said, "Let me ask you a question first."

I nodded.

"If I accept the light, will you Christians forget about me?"

I sat, stunned, for a second. Nobody in my thousands of visits and conversations in youth prisons had ever asked me that. I wasn't going to lie, so I could only sit and consider. The weight of this righteous question proceeding from a tormented little girl's soul was so strong that I trembled at responding.

She added: "Because he won't forget about me. And he'll come back."

She meant the demon assigned to her. I had never been in a conversation so sacred and so real.

"Christy," I finally said, "I can't answer for all Christians, but I promise you I will never forget you and I will always tell people about you."

She nodded with a pleasant kind of expression—or at least so it seemed.

"Okay," she said. "That's good enough for me."

"Let's pray," I said, but was thinking, *Lord, I don't know what to say right now. I need the words.*

I could sense the guards at either end of the hallway watching and perhaps hoping something good would happen. They had removed all other inmates from the area because they knew this was serious business and something important might happen. Now we were at a moment of decision. Christy and I sat across from each other at the wide-open cell door. She grabbed three of my fingers with her hands. I noticed how small her hands looked next to my big mitts.

"Father, I pray right now for Christy," I began. "I take authority over the darkness that has been in her life. I plead the blood of Jesus over this cell and over her. I command all forces of darkness to leave and have no more authority or influence over her life."

Suddenly, her body arched up sharply and she started squeezing my fingers with supernatural strength. I wondered half-seriously if I should speed up the prayer to avoid injury. Her hand cranked down on my fingers, but I wasn't about to pull them away. Whatever I suffered, I would suffer. She was worth it.

Then, just as suddenly, she went limp. Her body slumped forward. Her hair fell down over her face. It was quiet and still. I saw big tears fall from her eyes and splash onto her jumpsuit. She was free.

We finished the prayer, talked a little more, and then I walked out, telling her I would visit her again if I were ever at that facility. As it turned out, I never was. But I kept my promise to her.

Later I met with Christy's biological mom, son, and probation officer. I asked them about everything Christy had told me. They confirmed every detail of what she had said.

Countless kids in normal society and behind bars need hope and deliverance. As Christians, and as men, we are obligated to ask ourselves, *What are we doing for these kids? How are we helping single moms and widows? How about the fostered and fatherless?* The Bible is clear about what we owe people in these circumstances. When the Father asks you what you did for "the least of these," what will you tell Him? I'm asking you to think it through now, in advance of that most important conversation.

I can almost guarantee you there are needy kids and families within ten miles of where you live. There are probably youth prisons within 150 miles of where you live. I'm not saying you're called to youth prison ministry like I was, but if you are, you would fulfill two of Jesus's admonitions: caring for orphans and visiting prisoners. I consider this to be the neediest, most vulnerable population in the United States.

What I am saying, loudly, is that you must do *something*. It's not enough to "like" the right social media posts or give money to certain causes. Those are good things, but what have you done to personally impact the life of an individual in trouble? Is there a young man or woman who can say you made a pivotal difference in his or her life? If not, why not?

I'm not trying to pull a guilt trip on you. But in a time of emergency, as anyone on a plane knows, you have to get your own safety in order first before you can help others. Right now, the first order of business is building and protecting our own families—but we can't stop there, and God won't let us. When we're stable and strong enough, we must use our energy to put others on firm footing as well. That's how strong communities are built. That's how Jesus comes to rescue people.

Real change will happen when we do the right thing. And it can go well beyond helping an individual in a cell or a group of kids in a prison pod.

After I had ministered in prisons for a few years, a network of youth incarceration facilities in the South named me its Volunteer of the Year. It was a nice award and it signaled that All Things Possible was transforming lives. But then something unexpected happened: Huge amounts of corruption and perversion began coming to the surface throughout the network. I hate to even say this, but there were prison staffers engaging in sexual activity with kids. One kid allowed a warden to abuse him because he had given him a birthday cake, which the kid had never had in his life. Suddenly we saw people on the news being arrested, warden after warden, guard after guard, in a youth prison system that had won national awards for having "the highest standards." The swamp was being drained.

It was awful to watch. But when God began to capture the hearts of thousands of kids and bring them to Himself, light flooded in, drove out darkness, and exposed what was going on. The kids got bold enough to speak about what was happening to them in secret. As a result, that network was completely dismantled, and its facilities were emptied of children and repurposed to house adult inmates.

I will be the first to say, I didn't expect that kind of darkness to be exposed after God sent revival to those institutions. But it happened. It's part of the history of youth prisons in that state.

While it tells us that the Gospel is far more powerful than any one of us, it also tells us the Gospel needs someone to carry it into the darkest places so it can do its work. You were chosen before the foundations of the world to bring the light to someone, somewhere—to be dangerous to darkness. How is that going for you?

CHAPTER 6

IRAQ MINISTRY

On our second trip to Iraq, Chaz and I were standing behind an embankment in the city of Sinjar, looking at some ISIS-controlled buildings about a thousand yards away. It had been a relatively peaceful day with little gunfire and few explosions nearby. I was still surprised we could get so close to enemy-occupied territory as I watched the ISIS flags wave menacingly in the breeze.

"Chaz, record me. I'll make a video before we leave," I suggested.

Chaz pulled out his phone and tapped the screen. I hopped up onto the embankment and started ad-libbing a little report about our visit to share with family members and ministry supporters back home.

"Hey, we're here in Sinjar," I said. "It's relatively safe—"

As soon as I said that, a bullet whizzed past us. Chaz and I both ducked fast and scrambled behind the embankment, laughing.

"Someone must have seen us," he said.

A sniper in the building was obviously paying attention. Once safely behind the breastworks, I recorded a short video devotional, and then we moved on. A little while later, ISIS attempted a full-frontal attack on the spot we had occupied, complete with vehicles and bombs. It got nasty and a bunch of ISIS guys died as the Kurds held the position valiantly. Years later,

Dave installed a children's playground there as a symbol of rebirth and peace. But at that time, our ministry in Iraq was just beginning.

Eileen and I began planning our second trip to Iraq as soon as we returned home from the first one. We still didn't know what we would do there, but we had a strong sense that God assignments awaited us, and we were ready to help however we could. On the ground in Kurdistan that second time, we visited people we'd met and surveyed the landscape to see how our ministry might be useful. Most of all, we prayed, always asking, "Lord, what do You have for us here?"

Just getting our minds around the scope and scale of needs was a massive undertaking. Even if a thousand new ministries and NGOs had suddenly started operating, there was still a lot for us to do. The main reason others didn't join us is that in Kurdistan, everything and everyone was under constant threat of attack from ISIS. Our team had to keep moving and stay unpredictable, making plans and getting from one place to another with all the strategy of chess players before each move. We had to assume that ISIS had eyes everywhere—and would be especially interested in nabbing some Americans for propaganda purposes. Eerily, we saw no other Americans in the areas we visited—not even journalists or NGO workers.

From the beginning, God opened doors that never would have opened without Him. Our contacts introduced us to KRG intelligence officers and commanders in the area, and though they were cautious at first, we sensed we had some favor with them. My background in martial arts and weapons training may have helped, along with our work with veterans, but the KRG guys were battle-forged warriors. Stories of karate-kicking bags in dojos or teaching suburban families how to shoot a target in the woods would not impress them. Besides, I wasn't there to fight but to encourage the people doing the fighting while serving the dispossessed and fatherless. We wanted to do our best to assess their needs and hear their stories. We found ourselves listening a lot.

Before we went home, military personnel took us to see mass graves left by ISIS. It was horrible: hundreds of bodies buried in shallow graves, mostly just bones and hair by then, plus scattered AK-47 casings, shoes, and clothing. As gruesome as it was, the sight didn't trouble me terribly ... until I saw the bones of a child. Without thinking, I knelt down and picked up a small strip of cloth stained with dried blood that was tied in a circle, and then realized this was one of the rags ISIS used to tie kids' hands behind their backs before they shot them. That level of evil is, thankfully, unusual in our world, and the sudden pain of that realization stayed with me for a long time.

Going in, I knew about as much about ISIS as the average American did at that time. They were the latest boogeymen in the Middle East, the edgy new jihadists, and certainly their methods were more shocking and barbarous than those of al Qaeda or other terrorist organizations. But there on the ground, with ISIS firing live rounds at us, I learned more about their methods—and grew to hate them passionately. ISIS attracted the world's biggest perverts and most violent psychopaths. Their appetite for sexual abuse and physical torture knew no bounds. When foreign fighters joined them, ISIS guys would take them into a room, violate them sexually, videotape it and say, "If you ever cross us, we will send this to your parents." These were not "holy" people in any sense of the word. They were depraved, demonized souls on missions to kill and destroy until they themselves were destroyed. The mass grave was just one testament to that fact.

We spent that night in a bunker dug into the ground. Bunkers were everywhere and were built for operational use, not for living quarters. They were primitive and reinforced with sandbags, having doors but no windows. You had to walk hunched over inside of them, but they did have electric lights. When people heard the sound of mortars, they ran into the bunkers. While we were there, the sound of mortars and gunfire was constant on some days, so the bunkers were well used.

Thoughts of that strip of cloth had gotten to me, and that night I recorded a pretty emotional video in the bunker. It was the first time in Iraq that I could hardly contain what I was feeling, and it had to do with seeing dead children and thinking about my own kids back home. I hit that breaking point that soldiers and police officers and first responders have all experienced—the point when a scene of horror becomes personalized. Had I been born in Iraq, those could have been my kids in that grave. On top of that, I could feel God's love for the Iraqi people, and I ached to help them. It challenged my perspective as an American and as a minister. Could Eileen and I ever come to a place where we laid down our lives for these people— perhaps literally?

Meanwhile, the Kurds were fighting what seemed to them to be a forgotten war. "We're not just fighting for our town or land, but against the greatest evil in the world," they told us repeatedly. "We are fighting for you all, for the world."

At the time, Americans were tired of wars in the Middle East, and the United States government wasn't sending much help. Under the next presidential administration that would change, but at the time, the Kurds felt hung out to dry. Nobody seemed to appreciate the fact that ISIS was a form of evil several orders of magnitude beyond Al Qaeda. To Americans jaded by Western news outlets, they were just another jihadi movement.

Perhaps my biggest personal takeaway from that trip was that, apart from the difficulty of seeing those kids in the mass grave, I felt at home in that environment. When I saw the clashing of armies and heard the sounds of war, when I felt the chaos and smelled the destruction—I felt made to minister there. I'm not saying my reaction was normal. As I mentioned earlier, I experienced a lot of violence at an early age, and later joined the military. I don't get a thrill out of violence. I actually do everything I can to stop it or avoid it. Much of my life has been about minimizing and managing violence.

But this feeling of comfort in chaos spoke to something beyond my natural self. In that zone, I had a sense of divine purpose, a strong conviction that God would allow me and our teams to alleviate some of the suffering and shame there and to share the Gospel of Jesus Christ. I felt I was in the bull's-eye of God's will, certain that He had ordained me and our teams to work there for such a time as this.

Once back at home, we immediately began planning our third and subsequent trips. The wind was at our backs as God guided our decisions and brought the right people to us in Iraq and in the United States.

Working in Chaos

The central question, of course, remained: What would we do in the Middle East? It was such a different field than youth prisons, men's conferences, and church meetings. Clearly, we were pursuing a humanitarian mission, but that's a big, broad term. The goal of our ministry had long been to rescue people physically, spiritually, and emotionally from darkness. What did that look like in such an unstable non-Western environment? Would we simply supply goods and basic necessities as other NGOs did? Was our assignment purely to provide post-trauma counseling for former captives?

The more we prayed about it, the more we felt we should not limit our work to what other groups were doing or what had been done before. We recognized that we brought to the assignment a unique mix of strengths. For example, the security teams we brought in were made up of experienced combat veterans—guys who weren't afraid to fight as long as it was to defend innocent people or themselves as they served others. As we leaned into the question, we felt that God had designed our lives and teams for special tasks that would occur in the context of war.

Our learning curve was so steep and fast that sometimes I thought I would pass out from the g-force. A couple of things hit us right away: First, as eager as we were to help, and as capable as we felt in some areas, nobody in Iraq really knew us. Therefore, they had no reason to partner with us. Their hands were full already without an unknown ministry stepping into their space and trying to get involved. Trust is everything, and God would have to provide the relationships and the trust in His timing. There was no substitute for that.

Second, even to be mobile in that arena required us to meet with Iraqi leaders to receive the paperwork that would get us through checkpoints. That meant spending half a day with people in authority, having tea, getting to know them, and letting them see who we were. If they liked us, they gave us paperwork that said we were part of a trusted NGO and allowed to go wherever we needed. That still didn't mean they trusted us fully, or that we got through every checkpoint with ease. Every time we approached one of those concrete barriers with gun-toting guards ready to inspect our credentials, we had to remain confident and prayerful. If the guards balked at us, sometimes we had to call their superiors to persuade them to let us through. We also learned to raise our voices a little and assert the rights outlined in the paperwork. And honestly, sometimes we had to bribe people. But we never blamed them for being cautious. Violence was everywhere, and they wanted to make sure we weren't ISIS or just careless Westerners who would divulge locations and sensitive aspects of their missions through the media or social media. (Did I mention that ISIS had a strong, top-tier social media presence and knew how to scour posts for valuable information? The things you learn.)

With all that said, we also found, paradoxically, that the crazier the situation, the easier it could be to get through checkpoints. Paperwork, at times, went by the wayside. That was one "advantage" of chaos—it freed us from protocols. When bombs and bullets were incoming, dotting i's and crossing t's didn't seem to matter so much.

The Generals

As we visited frontline areas, we realized that our first hurdle to doing any kind of work was the generals, none of whom wanted us there—at least initially. There isn't a single qualified military leader who likes unknown foreigners hanging around his battlefield. This is true even if you come with a bunch of supplies and a desire to be useful. We knew we arrived with no credibility, and we understood that the generals would want us gone. I wouldn't have respected them if they didn't. We got used to explaining over and over again who we were and why we were there, as succinctly as we could.

Without Dave Eubank, I don't think our Iraq ministry would have gone anywhere. Dave is not only friendly, but more tenacious than any other human on the planet. He taught me the value of sticking around, smiling while insisting on being there, building relationships by proximity, and pressing through every "no" to achieve an outcome that benefited innocent people. I believe he is specially gifted at this, but it's also a skill that the rest of us picked up by his example. Did his relentless tenacity bother gatekeepers at times? Yes, of course. Did it work? Big-time. But it wouldn't have if he hadn't been so nice about it. It's rare and disarming to be confronted by a genuinely friendly person who will not take "no" for an answer, and that was one of the major skills we learned.

Slowly, with the aid of supplies and vehicles and a certain fearlessness, we were allowed to start delivering water and food to hotly contested territories where no other NGO dared to go. Seeing our courage under fire, the Iraqi generals and commanders tested us repeatedly to see if we were willing to do various things. Would we, for example, retrieve a bunch of civilians from a dangerous area when bullets were flying? Bit by bit, without acknowledging it verbally, generals began to treat us as informal partners who could do useful things they didn't have time to do, like supply newly liberated families with water, food, and medical care in parts of town the bad guys still wanted to control.

There was no model for what the Lord was asking our team to do, except what Dave had done in Burma. The war zones we found ourselves in were not the kind where NGOs, even medical ones, moved about freely to treat the wounded and evacuate the innocent. ISIS and other terrorist groups didn't stop shooting for anyone. To reach the stranded, as we were increasingly called on to do, our team had to gear up for battle. In fact, if we weren't set up as a combat unit, we would have failed every time and essentially delivered our goods to the bad guys—or become casualties or prisoners ourselves, with no one to rescue us.

In all this, we were limited in what we could do. It is illegal for an NGO to be involved in any aspect of waging war on foreign soil. If an organization is found to be operating that way, it puts all other NGOs in harm's way. Our teams had no official connection with the Iraqi government; we were not serving as mercenaries in their militias or any such thing. Likewise, our ministry never received any funding or support from the United States government. We were just a bunch of trained combat veterans and humanitarians making a difference in violent areas where other relief organizations wouldn't—or couldn't—go.

But we couldn't behave like conventional Special Forces with QRFs, satellites, great comms, and the best weapons. Tactically and communicationally, every nerve in my Marine Corps body at times was like, "Ahh! I can't believe we're doing this." It was unconventional and completely unsafe. Yet time and again, God blessed our efforts and protected us, body and soul. We knew by inner witness and outer evidence that we were called to do a special kind of work.

More quickly than we expected, relationships formed, connections were made, and assignments began to fall into our laps.

"Victor, you have the favor of God on your life because you give God all the glory," Eileen told me during those days. "Once people get to know you, it's not a stretch for them to go, 'It's God, not Victor.'" That was one of the most humbling compliments I received.

Soon, we had a large network of in-country partners and had forged actual relationships with great men and women there. They remain some of the best, most trustworthy people I have ever known. Cautiously but deliberately, we also began to use social media to tell people back home what we were doing, and this brought connections in the Middle East as well. Not only did God quickly ramp up our work, it seemed He also raised our profile higher than we expected—which led to more opportunities and fruitful connections of various kinds.

Eileen and I were so committed to our work in Iraq that we even took out a long-term lease on a house to live in during our quickly expanding time there. Elsewhere, our team set up a base of operations and put together an armory of weapons and military-grade vehicles, in addition to large amounts of practical supplies and ministry resources that became vital to our efforts over the years.

The Push into Mosul

Within a year or two of our first trip, several members of our team found ourselves in combat situations while on various assignments to help innocent people. It wasn't the only thing we did, but it was an important part of the whole. Depending on the mission, I might take four or eight guys in with me. We normally didn't take more than two or three vehicles. We trained in defensive tactics in the United States beforehand. Our missions varied from safely going into IDP camps to bring trauma relief to rescuing innocent people newly liberated from areas formerly controlled by ISIS. After each mission, we moved to the next location and did it again, repeating that over and over to the point of exhaustion.

Ideally, nobody died in our operations—not on the ISIS side, and not on ours. We were fully capable of dealing death, but what I really wanted was to take the Gospel to everyone—bad guys included. We didn't go into combat zones to kill people; we went to rescue and help people. Sometimes the latter required doing the former. But shooting people did not appeal to me, and eagerness for violence did not impress me. Yes, ISIS had chosen to wage war on innocent populations, killing the men and raping and enslaving the women and girls, and in making that choice, they gave up the right to peace and longevity. If ISIS interfered with my mission to bring aid and comfort to their victims, I would most certainly use my gun to hurt their feelings. But our goal was to be like King David, snatching victims from the jaws of bears and lions. That is what drove me: that irresistible urge to rescue women and children from dangerous people and situations.

Dave and I were told we were the only Americans embedded with the Iraqis on the initial push to take Mosul back from ISIS. By that time, Iraqi generals not only tolerated us but used us readily. Dave and I operated together at times, and also did a lot on our own—he with the Free Burma

Rangers and me with our All Things Possible teams. The villages the Iraqi Army was hitting at that time were all ISIS strongholds which had been gearing up for three years to defend against a big push from armored brigades, so this was serious business. Some of it was shown pretty graphically in a 2020 documentary about the Free Burma Rangers, but even that account, as awesome as it was, left out 95 percent of what we experienced.

One crazy moment came in a part of Mosul where Dave and his team had set up a FOB in a house that served as a distribution center for water and supplies. Dave either had more faith or was a lot crazier than I was, because I didn't like to stay in one place for more than a couple of days. He, on the other hand, set up a base at this house on a little street where other houses had been blown up—and he stayed there whenever he felt like it.

"It's totally safe, man. We're good here," he reassured me one night. "By the way, here's where you're sleeping tonight."

I thought, *Man, I won't be getting any sleep, but thanks.*

Some unknown Iraqi guys had gone to the house earlier to get water, and then they came back to ask for more. That is suspicious behavior, so some of the Iraqi guys in the military group we were embedded with went looking for the dudes—and found them three houses down, planning an attack on our house. They killed them on the spot.

Before we left, for some reason, I walked down the street and was surprised to see the dead ISIS guys still lying everywhere. That's how it was then; nobody took time to say, "What should we do with these bodies?" They left them in the house to rot, or maybe dug a shallow grave if they were in a public place.

Child Rescue

One of our tasks during those days was to respond when generals called us before or during a battle. One day we were in a safe house when a general called us from a live firefight.

"Families are running out of the buildings, and they need help," he said.

We kitted up, got in our vehicles, and drove into the fray. Everywhere we went in those vehicles, we risked being attacked. Every checkpoint, every road, every intersection, every house could become the site of an ambush. We would ride along watching for threats, checking our AK-47s, grenades, pistols, and ammo in case defensive action became necessary.

It usually played out this way: The Iraqi Army mounted an offensive to take a building, block, or village. Bombs would start going off everywhere, gunfire rat-a-tatting from every corner, dust and junk filling the air. You'd hear yelling, loud war-machine engines, missiles streaking through the sky. ISIS guys would start firing back, revealing their positions. You could see them and their weapons in windows, on rooftops, and behind the corners of buildings. Soldiers would be dying on both sides, and then you'd see innocent people running from the besieged buildings or village trying to reach safety. That's where we came into the picture.

When fighting starts, innocent people flee. Naturally, they don't want to be where bullets are flying and buildings are collapsing. But in addition, those folks wanted out of the hellish terrors of ISIS World. Some had been held captive and abused. Some were simply families whose lives had come under the cloud of war. They would make a break for it across the battlefield to try to get behind Iraqi Army lines. Here's the tough thing: When innocent people fled, ISIS gunned them down. Adults were easiest to hit, and that would leave children, sometimes just infants, crying on the ground in the middle of a battlefield next to their parents' dead bodies. Cruelly, ISIS would try to shoot these children as well, aiming for certain parts of their bodies without mercy.

Imagine standing alongside Iraqi Army guys, seeing those crying children—or people of any age—stuck in no man's land. Imagine knowing, as we did, that ISIS attracted some of the most experienced warriors in the world—veterans of Chechnya and elsewhere, many of them skilled shooters. Then imagine God saying to your heart, "Go rescue that child. Go rescue that woman." As strange as it sounds, I never felt hesitation to obey. I always felt a great sense of honor in it. That said, it is a unique feeling to sprint in open daylight toward someone, at times with no real protection, as guys on the other side try to take you down while you grab your person and drag or carry him to safety. Whenever the terrain was suitable, we used armored vehicles to reach them. Other times we went to positions our side had just taken and pulled known survivors from the rubble before they died of injuries. One general told me we were with him in one of the most dangerous, bloody battles he had ever experienced.

It didn't take many missions like this for us to gain the respect, trust, and love of militias and Iraqi Army units alike. Our sole goal was to save innocent lives, and God was letting us do just that.

"It's Too Much"

Still, it wasn't like Eileen or I had eased into this lifestyle through intermediate levels of danger and suffering. God took us straight from what we'd been doing in the United States to an advanced level in a theater of war. I don't recommend doing that unless He leads you, because it can be overwhelming. Like David, I tried to surround myself with mighty men and women, people who did things better than I did. But it was still jarring and disorienting to go from American church-based ministry and youth prisons to the frontlines of actual combat in the Middle East.

"It's too much, God," I prayed many times. "It's too much uncertainty. Nobody's doing this. Help us, Lord—I don't know if we can sustain it."

In some moments I struggled with fear so badly that I didn't know if I could go on—usually before I went to Iraq and after I got home. For whatever reason, I never felt afraid when I was actually there. But I frequently reminded God that I didn't set out to build a high-risk ministry, and I never once requested to go to combat zones. I was just trying to be a disciple, an obedient follower of Christ. When He says, "Follow me," you do it. You get out of the boat. You go where He goes.

Not once did I ever regret being there or say to myself, "We're in the wrong place. What are we doing?" It always felt right. It always felt good. It always felt like the Lord.

One thing was certain: I sure wasn't trying to make a name for myself on the Christian ministry circuit.

CHAPTER 7

THE DANGEROUS WIFE

What kind of woman not only goes with her husband into an active combat zone, but sets up a home there for her family? That would be Eileen, my fearless, selfless, queen-warrior wife. (Yes, I give her titles like that because it bugs her.)

Eileen is like no other woman. As kind and godly as she is, she can flip a switch and be one of the most violent, physically deadly people you've ever met. She has a black belt in karate, is a former Miss Fitness USA, and is a combatant who can shoot any pistol or rifle you put in her hand, drive any vehicle, put on a kit, and properly use night vision. She is almost sixty, has given birth to five children, and still has a six-pack. There is nothing normal about the woman I married.

Sometimes I am actually the moderate one in our partnership. I'll see Eileen with a faraway look in her eye, and then she'll come back to reality and share with me her latest creative idea for killing bad guys. I have to tell her, "Honey, you're getting pulled into darkness. Come back to the light."

She comes by it honestly: Her dad was a Marine who served in the Korean conflict. But like a lot of guys, he came back angry, drank heavily, and beat her mother. Understandably, Eileen never wanted to depend on a

man when she grew up, never trust a man, never give her heart to a man—
and she didn't until she met me.

It's hard for me to believe I was just twenty when we met, and she was
only twenty-three. I first saw her at church in Southern California. A friend
had invited her; Eileen wasn't a Christian, but she listened to the Bible teaching and was intrigued. She started attending church regularly and eventually
gave her life to the Lord, but one of her biggest hesitations about Christianity was the idea of women submitting to men in any way. "Uh, that ain't
gonna fly," she said. "I saw my mom do that, and it didn't turn out great."

I loved Eileen the first time I saw her, and the Lord spoke clearly to my
soul that she would be my wife. I still have the journal where I wrote that
down. I wanted to marry her right away (though I didn't tell her that), but
she was in a quasi-relationship with some other dude, the pastor's brother—a total idiot. For a year I had to suffer watching her try to make that
relationship work.

Then one day Eileen dropped by church on a weekday evening. Nobody
from the staff was there, but I was volunteering and doing some tasks around
the place. She looked as distraught as Eileen would allow herself to look,
which was not overly.

"Where are the pastors?" she asked me. "I need advice from a pastor."

"They're not here," I said. "Can I help?"

She must have been desperate because she laid out the problem for me
right there. "I'm dating this guy, but he wants to party, and he's supposed to
be a Christian," she said.

My literal words were, "He is the spawn of Satan. You must drop that
dude immediately."

It was the truth and, of course, I had an ulterior motive. I told her,
"Eileen, I'm actually looking for a wife. I don't want to date. I want to marry."

She gave me a look that said, *What a sweet thing to say, buddy, pal, friend,*
then said out loud, "You're such a nice guy. That's so great."

We parted. I wasn't sure she had gotten a lot out of my "counsel," but I was really hurting. I hadn't gained an inch of ground with her.

I was surprised when Eileen called me at 5:30 the next morning before her aerobics class.

"Victor, I want to make sure I didn't hurt your feelings," she said, and started crying.

Well, this is new, I thought.

"I want you to understand, I have to try to figure things out with my boyfriend," she went on. "I have to make sure he's not the one God has chosen for me."

"Yeah, sure, I get it," I said, trying to sound reasonable, manly, stoic— but I was in turmoil.

A whole year went by before she dropped that clown for good and circled back to me. She was teaching aerobics at my karate school and had been so on-again-off-again toward me that I wasn't sure I wanted to expose my heart to pain again. It did feel good to think she might be checking me out as a prospect. At the time, I was considering a huge job offer from Brian Wilson of the Beach Boys, who wanted me to serve as his personal assistant and security guard. I decided to do a test run of vulnerability by telling Eileen about it. I hadn't told another soul.

"So?" she said, unimpressed by the possibility of my stepping into the world of the rich and famous. "Did God tell you to take it?"

The fact was, God had told me *not* to take it, but I was hemming and hawing because it would have been such a huge jump for my career. Eileen's clarity was refreshing and admirable. I turned down the job, and now I was determined to make a relationship work with Eileen.

It so happened that some country cousins of mine from Louisiana were going to visit me in California, and I asked Eileen to go with us to SeaWorld—hugely romantic, I know. Up to that point, she and I hadn't shown any physical affection toward each other, not even holding hands. I'll never forget the moment in the SeaWorld penguin exhibit when I said to myself, *Just grab her hand. Let this be the first contact.*

Finally, I got up the nerve to say, "Eileen, may I hold your hand?"

"Yes, of course," she said, and then gave me the greatest compliment I had ever received: "Victor, I have never dated a gentleman."

Wow! In her eyes, I was a gentleman. Talk about positive reinforcement. I decided on the spot to be a gentleman to this woman for the rest of my life. I considered her the most valuable jewel in all the world. How could anybody *not* treat her with anything but the utmost respect and kindness?

I proposed to her that very month after a karate demonstration we did together. We were strolling on the back side of Strawberry Peak by Big Bear Lake, where there is an expansive view. I pulled a stalk of grass from the ground and rolled it into a ring. I didn't have any money for a diamond ring, but I knew I wanted to propose to Eileen. I knelt down and put one knee in the dirt.

"Would you grow old with me?" I asked.

She started laughing—full on. In my face. That was not the response I was looking for.

"Oh, my gosh, you're serious," she finally said.

"Yes, I want us to grow old together and walk with the Lord," I said. My heart was trying to beat its way out of my chest, maybe to flee the embarrassment.

"Of course," she said, in that gentle, strong way only Eileen has. She kissed me and hugged me, and I had never been so happy in my life. She was happy, too. In fact, she wore that grass ring for ten days and showed it to everyone, announcing, "We're engaged!"

Then the grass portion of the ring—which was all of it—fell apart, and Eileen asked me, "Now that we're engaged, doesn't it mean that your stuff is mine?"

"Yes," I said.

"And anything I have is yours?"

"Yes," I said.

She paused a moment, then said, "I have some money in an account."

"Okay," I said, then felt like I should ask, "How much?"

She told me the amount. It seemed like a lot, but money didn't impress me any more than fame impressed her. She had received a cash prize for winning the Miss Fitness USA contest.

"Okay," I said. "What about it?"

"My point is, it's yours. It's ours," she said. "Do you want us to go get a ring?"

Ahh, that was it. "Sure," I said. So we picked out a ring together, buying it with her cash prize money.

"I'll pay you back," I told her.

"There's nothing to pay back. It's our money," she said.

I had a lot to learn. (Later in life I did buy her a mega-ring, as well as the really nice watch she gave away in Iraq in exchange for that very valuable iPhone I mentioned earlier.)

But before our wedding, the effects of my, shall we say, "unusual" childhood roared back with a vengeance.

Up to then, every day with Eileen had been bliss. We sent out wedding invitations. We planned stuff. We couldn't believe we were actually getting married! But one day she came over to my apartment and, unlike any other time, I felt nothing. No joy, no happiness, no sadness, no anger. My emotions were in neutral, and I couldn't make sense of it.

"Are you okay?" she finally asked. "What's wrong?"

"I don't know," I said. "I just can't feel anything."

"Are you getting nervous about getting married? Are you getting cold feet?" she asked.

"It's not cold feet," I said. "I just don't care anymore. I can't feel anything. Right now, it doesn't matter to me if we marry or don't, or if I live or die. Nothing matters. I have no emotions."

Of course, Eileen started crying because of my words. She didn't know how messed up I was. The only hint she'd gotten had come a few days earlier when we were sitting at my table planning the wedding and I got a call from the stepfather who had smothered me. He was in prison at the time.

"I couldn't believe what I saw and heard when you talked to him," Eileen told me later. "My big, Marine, black belt husband became like a child on the phone. You got small and I saw a fearful young kid."

Now she was standing in my kitchen, crying, while I felt nothing at all. We called my roommate, who was on staff at the church, and his wife gave us a psychiatrist's phone number. I called the psychiatrist right away so we could talk to him.

"Something's wrong," Eileen told him, and explained what was going on, as best as she could.

"Victor, tell me about your mom," the man said.

I rolled my eyes. *Really?*

"Hey, don't get into the mom issue," I said. "I don't buy any of that Freudian stuff."

"Okay, then let me ask you this: What's the longest you've ever dated someone?" he asked.

"Why is that relevant?" I retorted.

"Just answer. What's the longest you've dated anyone?" he repeated.

"Three months?" I guessed.

"And how long have you and Eileen been sweet on each other?" he continued.

"Three months," I said … and then it started making sense.

"You have a trigger defense mechanism to shut down at this point," the doctor said. "Tell me about your mom."

Now I was more willing to go there. "I don't know," I said. "She was married six times."

"Did she ever give you advice on women and dating?" he asked.

I thought about it before answering, "I remember being in sixth grade, and Mom was drinking a fifth of Jack Daniels straight from the bottle. She was in the hallway of our rental house, about to go on a date with some dude. She looked at me, drunk as a skunk, grabbed me, and pulled me close to her face and said, 'Don't ever trust a woman. They will only use you and leave you.' Then she pushed me away, slamming me against the wall. I grabbed the back of my head because it hurt. That was the only advice I received from my mom about dating."

It was clear to me now that I had believed her. How could I not? Her life had modeled exactly what she had said. The doctor hardly needed to weigh in on what was happening to me, and after the call, Eileen and I stood there alone in the quiet.

"Victor, I know you've got problems with your past," she said, "and I know you're scared and worried about me leaving you. That's the basis for your turning numb."

What she said next, I'll never forget, because it was the moment I knew she loved me.

"We're going to cancel the wedding. Not a big deal. We'll send a note to everyone saying we have to reschedule," she said. "But I'm not going anywhere. We will not get married until you're comfortable. If we're eighty-five years old and you say, 'I'm ready,' then we'll get married."

She said it with such authority and genuineness that I believed her. I hugged her and said, "You really do love me."

She said, "I do, and we will never divorce."

We did not cancel the wedding but kept our original date. It felt like God put a bubble of peace and joy around us that day. There was a newness, a shyness, a safety, and a blessing that has never left us. Yes, we were young in the Lord. I had been saved for two years, Eileen for just one. But we never doubted our commitment to each other. And I'll encourage you younger guys by saying that our intimacy after thirty-five years of marriage is just as innocent and exciting as ever, and it feels to me like opening a Christmas gift every time.

True love gets better and better in every way.

"I'd Rather Be a Widow"

From the start, I wanted to live up to Eileen's view of me as a gentleman. By that, I don't mean a harmless man-child, or a pasty dad-bod type. When

I looked around, it seemed the only danger a lot of men posed was to the high score of their favorite video game or the nearest bag of chips. I'm glad I married a woman who would not allow me to devolve into that kind of guy.

At the same time, Eileen had to come to a place of letting me lead our marriage. She had to conclude, "If Victor is following the Lord, he will love me the way I need to be loved. I can let him lead, as long as I know the Lord is leading him." That became her superpower in our relationship. She learned a long time ago that yelling at me, trying to get physical with me, or coming directly at me did not work. What works with me is her calm voice saying—in love, not aggravation—"Victor, lead me better than this." I feel it every time. She means, "You're better than this. You're a leader, the father of my children, my husband, a world-changer. You can climb mountains, swim oceans, and slay dragons, so right now just lead me better than what you're doing." It works like a shock collar on me. She wants me to be dangerous, but she also won't allow me to be anything less than a gentleman.

I believe this is what all women want. I've noticed publishing houses don't put wimpy guys playing video games on the covers of women's romance novels. They put super-muscular, powerful, passionate guys. The woman is always pictured in his arms, being held firmly, subject to his power—and yet the man is always touching her tenderly. It's not about violence; it's about protection and strength under control. Women want dangerous, gentle men.

Let's be 100 percent clear that I'm not talking about being violent in any way toward women. For a dangerous gentleman, there is never a time for roughing women up, keeping them in line, teaching them a lesson, or whatever stupid little macho phrase people use to justify sick, criminal behavior. There is no more massive display of male weakness than striking or mishandling a woman or a child. If I found out you did such things and you were in my presence, you would discover quickly that I was dangerous—toward *you*. Male power is for the protection and nurturing of women, children, and society.

But to help us strive for true manhood, I believe every dangerous gentleman needs a butt-kicking wife. (Not a wife who knows karate, necessarily, though it might help.) A good wife can be quiet and demure and meek and all that—but she'd better not let you get away with being anything less than the man you were made to be. Without Eileen, I would not be anywhere close to what God has called me to be. Guess what? Neither would you. (But with your own wife. Quit thinking about my wife. I'm serious.)

Eileen has talked me out of being a coward so many times, I don't even like to remember them. She enforces the standards of manhood. I even dress differently than I otherwise would because of her. Behind every great husband is a dangerous wife with a (figurative) knife at his back, pushing him to be the guy God created him to be.

But guys, women need to hear that they have permission to play that role. Some of you need to sit your wife and family down, apologize for being a pushover, say you're setting new standards for yourself, and that things are going to change. You're going to be braver in difficult decisions, more forthright about hearing from God and leading from that place of faith. You're going to be more of a leader—and you give them permission to hold you to that.

That'll change your entire household. And guess what? They will love and honor you for it.

Here's an example of how an empowered wife behaves. When we first got involved in Iraq and realized it was going to be dangerous, I brought up a tough subject with Eileen.

"Let's talk about the elephant in the room," I said. "Are you ready to be a widow for the cause of Christ? Because if I go into these combat areas with the teams, I could die. People are dying everywhere over there."

She looked at me without flinching and said, "I'd rather be a widow than be married to a coward."

Wow. This woman! I thought.

The subject didn't startle her, but her response caught me off guard. She had already put on her big-girl pants and settled the fact that we were heading into rough territory, and anything could happen.

Nonetheless, Eileen always insists I hear God's voice before every move, especially risky ones. Recklessness in the guise of bravery is not allowed. Her favorite line when I discuss anything—rescuing a kid, visiting a camp, meeting with Muslim leaders, whatever it may be—is, "Did God tell you to do it?"

I love that and I hate that. I sometimes bow up and respond, "I'm trying to hear His voice right now, woman!" But, of course, she's right and I wouldn't have it any other way.

I like what Eileen told a group of women one time: "I used to try to manage Victor. I'd say, 'Honey, don't get involved with that. It's too dangerous.' But ladies, it's when I finally opened the corral door and said, 'Run when you feel you need to run. I'm not here to control you,' that Victor began doing even greater things. Don't hinder your man. If it means he dies, then let him die valiantly."

Does your wife have permission to hold you to high standards of manhood?

Lions and Lambs

Eileen came up with a brilliant idea that turbocharged our effectiveness in the Middle East. After our first trip to Iraq, she mused, "The kids there had nothing to play with but dirt. We need some way to minister to them."

Among the things we had taken were a few dozen tiny stuffed animals—twenty-five lions and twenty-five lambs—that a donor had sent with us. The kids adored them. Now we ran with that idea: What if we made them bigger—more huggable? What if we put music in them—or, better yet, reassuring words and prayers? In fact, what if we really did it right and *created* music proven to calm people's anxiety?

We immediately started making calls and discussing possibilities. Chaz wrote Scripture-based reassurances and prayers that would be applicable in any culture (since these were not evangelistic toys), and we had these phrases and prayers professionally translated into Kurdish and Arabic. Then we added background music shown to bring a sense of peace and calm. My own kids narrated the readings.

After a year of development, our first shipment of Lions and Lambs arrived in Irbil via Turkey. Quickly, those stuffed animals became our secret weapon. When you squeeze a paw or a hoof, the animal talks. Countless times we watched kids listen to the message and music and begin holding the stuffed animal tighter, like, *You're not going to take this from me, right?* Everything about their countenance changed when they held it and listened.

Lions and Lambs turned us into something like Middle Eastern Santa Clauses, bringing stuffed animals, food, dignity kits with feminine products for women, and more to villages and camps. While All Things Possible gets a lot of attention for the high-risk missions we do around the world, the most effective tool we've ever had are those toys.

Fostering the Orphans

We didn't just put anxiety-reducing stuffed animals into the arms of thousands of children, though; we took some of those children into our own arms, too. Within a year or so of being in Iraq, Eileen and I began fostering orphans. Again, it was born from a need. When we rescued kids who had lost their parents or had been found under rubble, what were we supposed to do with them? There was no institution or organization in Iraq to receive them. Armies had no way to care for them. The only answer we could come up with when parents were gone, and relatives couldn't be found, was to take those kids into our own home.

That was the house we leased long-term in Iraq once we saw we would be spending weeks and months there each year. It was located in a gated neighborhood and had several bedrooms and bathrooms, a kitchen, and most everything else you'd find in a standard American home. When the power went out, generators kept the lights on. I was always concerned some entrepreneurial ISIS guy would get through and try to make his reputation by pulling off a hit against us, but that never happened. Having that house gave us the ability to start temporarily fostering orphans.

Our own kids stepped up in a big way to make that effort possible. We had begun taking them with us on some trips, and they shouldered a lot of the responsibility for feeding, playing with, and caring for these little individuals. We treated each one like he or she was our own child, our own brother or sister. They slept in cribs, on a mattress in our bedroom, or in the bed with us if they needed comfort. Some stayed for a few days, some for weeks. The oldest was probably seven; the youngest were infants.

As intense as it was fostering little kids in our own home, it also felt like one of life's great privileges to be the answer to a child's prayer for safety and nurture. I don't think Eileen and I ever even talked about it—we just knew it was right to shelter those kids until we were able to find their relatives or some longer-term place for them to live. We never even knew most of their real names, so we gave them new ones while they were with us.

Adopting them was never an option because that wasn't our role. We wanted to heal families by reuniting them whenever possible—but finding relatives often proved tricky. We had to protect the kids from possible kidnappers and ISIS members, so we would put out the word that we had kids, then do very strong background checks on relatives who showed up to claim them. Once we felt certain a child belonged to that family, we released him or her, but continued checking on them for several months, sending teams to visit and see if they were doing well.

Before releasing them, we spent time with their families. Many nights I saw Eileen dancing around the house, bouncing a baby on her hip to keep it happy. She sang to the orphans of that war. We stayed up with them, reassuring them, feeding them formula, changing their diapers. The hardest part for me was when they gave that particular soul-scream that said they somehow knew their parents weren't coming back. That's a sound you wish didn't exist—but it does, and the memory of it still haunts me.

Our house in Iraq also hosted a group of mothers who had been kidnapped and forced into sex slavery. In fact, those mothers were reunited with their children at our house, with a great many tears. The local intelligence agencies involved told us something about the women that surprised us: "You'd better have high security and big guns, and as soon as you can get them out of here to a different location, do it."

"Why?" we asked. "Will ISIS come for them?

"No," they said. "Their own families will try to find them and kill them because they have been tainted and used."

That was another horrible reality. Depending on the situation, women violated by ISIS often could not return to their families and tribes. Even their babies—and this is truly evil—would be thrown into a lake by their own relatives to drown. Despite the horrors they faced, some rescued women would later return to ISIS to save their own lives or their children's.

Nonetheless, we hosted women until they figured out where they could go to start life anew, regardless of what they chose. And that was all because of Eileen, who proved a masterful homemaker on two continents, in war and in peace.

And together, our adventures were just beginning.

CHAPTER 8

OFF THE MAP AT CAMP AL-HOL

H ey, boss, this dude's eyeing you."

Our team stood on the border of Iraq and Syria near the Tigris River crossing while an unknown man some distance away paid a little too much attention to us. Eileen had spotted him first and nudged me. Our security guys, who were walking an informal perimeter around our vehicles, noticed him as well. Hundreds of people were circulating in an open area that looked like a standard village bus stop with old, rickety, diesel-powered buses coming and going. Families were trying to get in or out of Iraq— mainly out— and Kurdish security forces were busy scanning for ISIS guys among the churning mass.

But this guy was clearly keying in on us. He looked like a normal Iraqi: nondescript slacks, sandals, a sweaty, long-sleeved, button-down shirt two sizes too big for him, and some kind of Arabic headwear. Nothing fashionable, nothing out of the ordinary … but nondescript guys can be just as dangerous as the ones screaming and carrying automatic rifles; sometimes even more so. His presence took us from high alert to even higher alert. Our security team was fully prepared to use their guns the moment it became necessary. So was I. So was Eileen.

"I'll shoot this guy if he comes anywhere near you," one security member told me as a way of getting my permission.

"Do it," I agreed.

As Americans, we were considered high-value targets. To compound the problem, in just a few years of ministering in Iraq, Eileen and I had become well-known throughout the Middle East. By that point, All Things Possible teams had visited many refugee camps, taken part in some hair-raising conflicts, and helped around forty thousand women and children find freedom for their bodies, minds, and souls. That got the attention of big Arabic television channels, which had featured our work in a very positive light. We were still one of the only American groups going over to help in that dangerous area, and Iraqis loved that we were doing large-scale trauma care for women and children affected by ISIS, not to mention rescues. More than once a local newsperson broke down crying while reporting on us. It was the presence of God, but they attributed it to the love we showed to the kids.

All of that added up to ISIS knowing who we were. ISIS hated all Westerners and Christians and wanted to send a message to the citizens of Iraq and beyond: *Don't work with these people.* To many Iraqi people, we were saviors, but to ISIS, we were nothing more than infidels.

The military situation in Iraq also had shifted dramatically since we began working there, mainly due to the election of President Donald J. Trump. As soon as he entered office, he smashed ISIS in a way the group probably wasn't expecting. Their illusion of total power was shattered. Tens of thousands of refugees—mostly women and children, some of them ISIS families—washed over the border into Syria, where large camps were established to house or confine them temporarily. The situation turned especially hairy as the border area was overrun by what some termed "zombie people"—refugees fleeing famine and destruction. The United States military withdrew from certain places rather than play desert police force, but we felt our ministry should go to the tough places—in this case, Syria, which was more or less in a state of anarchy. Someone had to bring hope and recovery to people who had just experienced Hell on Earth—even ISIS wives who supported the horrors their husbands were wreaking.

But first we had to get across the border, which was proving tricky—and now this unknown person was about seventy-five yards away and walking toward us. Our guys slowly placed their hands on or near their firearms. We never knew what was going through a stranger's mind, or what he might suddenly do. For all we knew, he might pull out a gun or detonate a bomb vest. He might be coordinating with multiple other people in a way we couldn't see. Anything was possible, and our response had to be swift; if he made a move on us, our guys would kill him first and ask questions later.

In fact, our team members were already flanking him, though he probably didn't notice it. His hands were visible; his shirt didn't look especially puffy with bombs, grenades, or anything else. There was no obvious pistol shoved down his pants. His gait was not that of a warrior; if anything, he would have been a sacrificial lamb. When he got within fifty yards of me and Eileen, our guys quickly approached, telling him to stop and getting ready to take him down bodily, if necessary.

The guy lifted his hands. "Wait, wait, please, wait," he said. "Friend, not enemy. Not ISIS—friend."

Then he squinted at me across the distance and asked our guys, "Is that Victor Marcus?" ("Marcus" is how Arabs pronounce my last name. I haven't been able to cure them of it.)

"Why do you want to know?" they demanded.

"I follow him on the Facebook, and we love him," the man said, his hands still above his head. "May I please meet him?"

My guys looked at each other, then moved in to check him thoroughly for weapons. Nothing. They put the guy between them and walked him up to me. The closer he got, the bigger his smile grew.

"Victor Marcus, I can't believe it's you!" he said. "Please, may I take picture?"

"You can if you promise not to post it until we leave," I said, hoping he understood what I was saying—and hoping he would comply with it. I didn't want him to compromise our position through a casual post on worldwide social media.

"Yes, yes," he said, then took selfies with me and Eileen with his cell phone. He walked away one happy guy, thanking our security team members who, of course, had been ready to gun him down if his interests hadn't been so benign.

A higher public profile was something our teams increasingly had to deal with; it came with the sudden favor God had given our ministry in that part of the world, and on the whole, it was a positive thing. But actually crossing the Syrian border was proving to be a bigger problem than our unexpected Facebook friend, and I didn't know how to solve it.

Border Crisis

Under my breath, I was blaming Dave Eubank.

"Victor, you need to go to Camp al-Hol," Dave had told me recently in that way that says, "Your life is about to change."

I don't know how Dave heard about al-Hol, but when he seizes on an idea, there's no shaking him loose from it. If Dave saw a portal to Hell and an opportunity to rappel down and save people, he wouldn't hesitate; he'd set the rope and convince you to go down with him. So I had agreed to venture well outside our normal working area and cross the Syrian border into a no-man's-land to visit one of the largest and most notorious confinement camps in the Middle East. And Dave wasn't even with us.

The obstacles to our success were many. We had few real contacts In Syria or at the border. It was like starting over with zero credibility. Nobody cared who we were or what we wanted to do. One guy among thousands might recognize us from Facebook, but overall, the persuasive power of our profile was proving limited.

Syrian border officials looking at our armored vehicles and weapons promptly said, "No way. You're not taking those in. You'll have to leave them here and we will hold them until you get back." They knew ISIS was operating everywhere in their country, attacking convoys, stealing whatever they needed and running roughshod over people and villages. There was no safe place to hide. Local law enforcement had disappeared. Famine was driving regular Syrian citizens to attack military outposts to try to keep from starving. It was the closest thing I ever saw to an apocalyptic *Mad Max* scenario. So five armored vehicles rolling up full of polite Americans asking to be allowed through for humanitarian reasons was a total nonstarter for them. They weren't even looking for bribes.

But armored vehicles and weapons had been the linchpin of our plan to get to and from our destination in Syria safely. We were going to wheel in with them and a truck full of supplies, head far into the desert about an hour from the camp, circle up, and create a little staging area. Our guys would patrol twenty-four hours a day so that if any vehicle or person came at us, we could obliterate them. The hope was that any bad guys attacking us would have less weaponry than we did.

Now that plan was toast because we would have no heavy vehicles and no guns, and we would be going into perhaps the most dangerous few square miles on the planet. We tried to convince the border guards, but they weren't yielding, so we pulled aside to a nearby vacant spot, parked, and got out of our vehicles to talk it over. We were faced with the less-than-awesome option of leaving tons of valuable military equipment at the border or turning around and going home with our tails between our legs. It was another reminder that you could spend $100,000 on a mission and not accomplish your objective.

I certainly was feeling the "no go, boss" from fellow members. Everyone knew this was likely a mission-killing event. To anyone with battlefield preparation or experience, the prospect of going into anarchic territory with no armored vehicles or guns was, to put it in official terms, nuts. My own Marine vibes were super-negative on crossing a border without protective equipment, but something in me wasn't ready to give up on the mission.

"What do you guys think?" I asked, opening the conversation.

"That's one of our policy markers: no vehicles, no weapons, no mission," one guy reminded us right off the bat. The silence that followed clearly told me no one was going to suggest going in anyway. But I didn't want to call things off yet.

After a few more scattered comments, none of them achieving any kind of cohesion, Eileen looked at me and said, "Let's take a walk."

Our guys posted up and she and I began walking, praying, and talking in the area near our vehicles. Other members of our team stayed in the vehicles themselves, praying earnestly. I thought Eileen would try to talk me out of going through with the plan, but soon found she was trying to talk me *into* it.

"Honey, we may never have the chance to get into Syria and reach all those ISIS people again," she said. "We have lions and lambs and your testimony book. I think we should risk it. I think it's God's will, regardless of what happens to us."

That was a definitive statement from my wife, but before even hearing her words, I had concluded the same thing.

"I think we go," she said.

"I do, too," I said, and after looking each other in the eyes for a moment as if to gauge our resolve, we headed back to the vehicles. The team circled up.

"We feel we ought to go," I said and let that sink in a minute. "This opportunity may never come back. But obviously, we'll have to change the plan. We're not going to do the wagon wheel in the desert because we won't have anything to defend ourselves with. But we think we can make it work with the resources and personnel we have, get to that camp with all those women and kids, and see what God wants to do."

After a moment, guys started to nod their heads, a good sign. Consensus quietly formed as everyone internalized the new, stripped-down, way-less-secure version of our assignment.

"Alright, let's do it," our team lead said. "Any objections?"

There were none, and the huddle broke. We had to transfer the stuff the Syrians were allowing us to take in—lions and lambs, copies of a kids' comic book containing my testimony, and basic supplies for ourselves—into Syrian vehicles. Then we waved goodbye to our armored vehicles and weapons, which we hoped would be in good hands with the Syrian police until we returned. I did manage to sneak in two weapons: a handheld tomahawk ax and Eileen's dog, Reagan. We had to bribe the border guards to get the dog across, but it was money well spent.

With that, we took a giant step of faith and put our lives in God's hands once again in entirely new territory.

Getting There

The day was mostly gone by the time we crossed the Tigris River and got into open country, and with the adrenaline wearing off, we had to work to stay alert. It would take another day to get to al-Hol, and we had to make up some mileage night-driving to keep to our schedule.

We jostled along for hours down dirty roads, hoping in the backs of our minds we would avoid the land mines reportedly placed on these "highways." Every time we saw another vehicle, we wondered if it contained ISIS raiders, and if they would turn around and try to smash up our vehicles, kidnap us, and take everything of value. That was the state of things in Syria then.

Our in-country contacts, whom we did not know well, had recommended a "hotel" we could stay in, and we arrived there by dirt roads around midnight. The Ritz it was not.

"Okay, everybody, we gotta move quick to get inside," our team lead said. In Syria, an attack could take place at any time. We also weren't real keen on being spotted, since this lodging was maybe 150 yards from where Syrian President Bashar al-Assad's military attachment was stationed. Had they known Americans were there, they would have apprehended us for sure. That's just the way things worked.

Whatever this building was, it wasn't even a one-star motel. The rooms reeked of cigarette smoke. Ashtrays on the tables encouraged the practice.

Toilets barely worked. Water from the faucet was a nice idea but not a felt reality. Worse, the place didn't have proper exits. There was one way in, one way out. That is not a warrior's favorite thing to discover in the dead of night when he's about to go to sleep.

Eileen and I were given a corner room on the second story. Visible from our window was the building directly across the street, about forty feet away, where we could clearly see people. That meant we had to keep the lights off, and because the ingress/egress situation was not favorable, we had to plan an escape route through the window, through which we would descend to a (we hoped) waiting vehicle by way of bed sheets and paracord I carried with me, if that's what it took.

One of our guys stayed in the lobby all night with a weapon he'd been able to smuggle over the border. And we had a dog and a tomahawk.

As usual, we all carried a certain amount of "escape money" to buy off kidnappers if needed. The ministry also had protocols to follow if a team member were kidnapped. This involved pushing it out on social media to draw attention to the situation and create an international incident.

It was unusual to feel vulnerable again. By that time, living in Iraq had come to feel more or less normal. Even in heightened security areas where car bombs went off, or someone was shot and someone else kidnapped, we found ourselves kind of shrugging it off. Fieldcraft and the four A's—awareness, assessment, avoidance, and action—had become a way of life.

We instinctively watched everyone around us, seeing who came in, who went out, and what they seemed to be doing. If a vehicle pulled up that seemed out of place, we all reacted without even discussing it. In any building we entered, we wordlessly knew all the exits and noticed anything peculiar.

But now we were in Syria, and Syria was essentially lawless.

Bone-tired, I lay there fully clothed in the dark next to Eileen. The four hours of sleep we got proved a victory. Then we were back in the vehicles, rumbling along for several more hours on our way to the mother of all ISIS confinement camps.

At the Camp

Camp al-Hol sat about thirty minutes from the nearest town. Officially, it was a refugee camp, but really it was more of a confinement center—a prison—for seventy-two thousand ISIS-affiliated women and children from Iraq, Syria, and fifty other countries. Oddly, it was overseen not by the United Nations, the United States, or even Syria, but by the Kurds.

Women and children were taken there after Iraqi armies captured ISIS cities and strongholds. Soldiers didn't want to shoot women or children, so they arrested and transported them. They remained in Syria because—small wonder—their home countries did not want them back. ISIS had been so effective at recruiting members worldwide that entire families from places like Europe, Australia, and Asia, even the United States—all Muslims, all radicalized—ended up in battle zones. It was weird to hear the occasional ISIS fighter or his wife speaking French, German, Japanese, or English.

They lived in tents at al-Hol and were divided into five sectors to keep the various nationalities more or less separate. Within that framework existed some not-really-committed ISIS-affiliated people, middle-ground ISIS people, and full-blown ISIS extremists, all mingled together. Some of the women, like their husbands, believed in taking over the world starting from a caliphate based in Syria and Iraq. Some had bombs strapped to their bodies inside the camp and were waiting for the best opportunity to blow themselves up. Others, particularly among the foreign women, just wanted to go back to their home countries—but if they even talked about leaving, loyal ISIS women would judge them and kill them in the camp. There had been more than a hundred murders there in eighteen months. ISIS guys were allowed to go in and out, ostensibly to visit their families but also to bring in money, weapons—and slaves. Women were complicit in hiding these activities. One time the camp operators raided an extremist section and found underground tunnels with sex slaves chained up below ground.

All of this explains why people freaked out when we told them we were going to al-Hol in the first place. But the Lord had shown us He gathered these people together in one spot so we could minister to them at one time instead of doing fifty-plus missions to people like them all around the world, which would have been impossible.

After passing through several checkpoints, we finally pulled into the camp with our vans, parked, and got ready to walk through yet another checkpoint. The camp director, a Kurdish woman, welcomed us. This was as far as our vehicles were allowed to go, so the team hopped out and began unloading the toys, comic books, and supplies.

So far, so good.

I hadn't seen the printed Arab-language version of my comic book yet, so I opened one up and thumbed through it. It was designed to share my testimony of going from darkness to light without using my name and without overtly presenting a Christian message. In these situations, we were not there to evangelize or talk about our ministry. Nothing we brought into the camps was designed to be a conversion tool; if I or my family were in a refugee camp or hospital in great need, I wouldn't want others taking advantage of my situation to try to convert me or my kids to their faith. We wanted to respect the people we encountered. There were other times and avenues for sharing the Gospel.

The comic book looked great, and I was proud that we were going to be giving away five thousand copies that day—but when I got to the back page, a feeling of horror swept over me. There in all its glory was our contact information: all our social media, our website URL, and a fairly specific geographic location for our ministry. None of that was supposed to be on the Arab-language version.

"Oh, my gosh—whoa, whoa, whoa. Don't unload anything!" I called out to the team. "We can't let even one of these get out!"

Eileen read my mood instantly. "What's wrong?" she asked.

"Look at this," I said, and handed her the comic book, open to the last page. "This is the most concentrated group of ISIS people anywhere in the world. All our contact info is in this book. We might as well give everyone our business card and invite them to our house."

She didn't look as alarmed as I felt.

"We've got to burn all five thousand of these," I went on. "Or maybe we just rip the back page off each of them."

Eileen was growing calmer as I grew more intense.

"Honey," she said, "we may not ever have the opportunity to share the Gospel this way through your testimony with five-thousand-plus ISIS families again. We need to give them out."

Her faith may have challenged me, but I was also questioning her sanity.

"You're willing to give our contact information, in a gospel comic book, that will reach ISIS people all over the world?" I said. "You're aware these people will study us. They'll track our movements as best they can from the information we publish. They may show up at our speaking engagements. They may even pay us a surprise visit somewhere."

Of course, they could have done that already, but then again, we hadn't distributed five thousand calling cards to the world's largest ISIS confinement camp before.

"Yeah," said Eileen, unshaken. "We should pass them out no matter the consequences."

Once again, my wife held us to a higher standard when I was far more inclined to be protective (or overprotective). I sighed, resolved myself to the level of courage necessary, and started carrying the books into the camp. That day, I may have become one of the most well-known Christians to Muslim extremists. I could hardly believe we were blanketing the place with the information, knowing that the threat would never really go away afterward. Those comic books could float around the Middle East for decades.

As usual, the lions and lambs were a huge hit with the kids. We talked with people, smiled, and took as much love and encouragement as we could to that isolated, forsaken place. More than that, God allowed us to make strong connections with the people who worked there, and within a short time our ministry became operational in that camp on a weekly basis. That meant sending in local teams to hold events for kids and families—everything from setting up a television to play biblically based cartoons to giving teachings on personal character and forgiveness. On holidays, our teams gave out tons of gifts to the children and families.

Again, the immediate purpose was less about conversion and more about earning trust with the women and caring for them in their circumstance. In that context, "conversion" meant death. Those people's families would kill them for leaving Islam. When people in any strongly Muslim culture want to follow Jesus, we tell them to be very sure of what they are doing. It's not simply a matter of changing your belief system and finding another spiritual community. They often have to leave their home, perhaps leave the country, and prepare never to see their family members again. In many cases it means starting life over.

For that reason, ministry in those places is not without consequences. Our point person there, a Syrian Christian woman, was attacked inside the camp once for being a Christian. That's to be expected, but then ISIS carried out a hit on her outside the camp. She was driving to al-Hol one morning when a big truck hit her head on, then drove away. The "accident" broke her body up and put her in a coma. When she came out of the coma, one of the first things she said to her daughter was, "Tell the All Things Possible team that as soon as I'm out of the hospital, I'm going back to the camp to continue the work."

She did just that, knowing she could die at any time.

Courage in the Culture

This is a good place to pivot and look at where most of us live as Americans. We may think our culture is safer than others, and that has historically been true, but it's becoming less true all the time. Leading people and institutions in our culture are at war with our values and our faith. They have categorized us as a threat, and in a manner of speaking, I think it's about time they did. Jesus's teaching absolutely threatens the authorities and powers of this world. It's almost like Christians weren't acting dangerously enough, so God showed the world that we are indeed a threat—or at least should be.

I notice that in the book of Acts, whenever Christian disciples showed up to share the Gospel in a new city, riots broke out and the people beat, stoned, and imprisoned them. Anyone who thinks the Gospel message will win favor with leaders and powers in our day is fooling himself. Soft-pedaling the message, couching it in terms to win converts ("How many did you lead to the Lord, brother?") rather than make disciples is shallow work. It's cowardly; not wise or clever. And who wants to join a movement that isn't bold and taking ground? The Gospel challenges dominant secular ideas in any era, at any time. I don't see one get-along Christian in the entire New Testament. I see social ostracization, decapitations, crucifixions, incarceration, and crowds driving people out of town. I see Rome, the world superpower of its day, mobilizing its government resources to silence the message.

Here in the West, if the secular institutions and the demonic forces controlling them are finally calling us dangerous, then why not just go ahead and be dangerous? Why not stand up the way the woman in that al-Hol camp did, risking her life? To use a really specific scenario, why not raise a hand in one of those mandatory diversity, equity, and inclusion meetings at your office and insist that your employer make space for people of religious conviction there? Why not speak openly against public schools when they teach perverse forms of sexuality to children? How can we *not* be bold? In a way, it's never been easier to be a dangerous gentleman than now, because our own culture has already declared war on us.

You know who is truly dangerous in American culture? Your company's human resources director and the government bureaucrats (at all levels) making regulations that dictate how we can live our lives, run our businesses and, yes, operate our churches. And how about the judges who change the definition of morality with a single ruling? They are boldly dangerous … and yet most Christian men remain far too gentlemanly. When's the last time you showed up at your child's school, talked with the principal and teacher, and let them know you'd be paying careful attention to what's taught in that classroom, and that you expect it not to violate your family's standards of morality? Would the consequence be any worse than what ISIS did to our friend in Syria?

When I think about our frontline worker at Camp al-Hol and countless others voluntarily living and ministering in truly dangerous situations, I go, "Really, American dad? You can't be bothered to attend that school board meeting and tell the leaders you won't allow them to teach smut to your kid? Because you're afraid someone might recognize you and you might lose your job? Or lose a few friends? What kind of pattycake are you?"

The only real requirement I have for people to be on our high-risk teams is courage. I will not jeopardize my life or anyone else's by having someone on the team who lacks physical courage and moral courage. I don't care what else you're good at—without courage, you're too dangerous to bring along.

That's true in America now, too. The future belongs to the courageous—the lions, not the sheep or the wolves. Celebrity pastors, feel-good Christian leaders, woke "Christian" apologists—those folks are quickly becoming irrelevant. Cowards tends to fade from view when the stakes go up. Bad people have decided to go all-in and be dangerously bad, and they won't be stopped until you and I become dangerously good.

Our team made it out of Syria alive the day after visiting al-Hol. We successfully reclaimed all our armored vehicles, weapons, and gear back at the border. But the biggest thing about that trip was what we left behind: an outpost of good news and hope in one of the darkest, deadliest places on Earth.

CHAPTER 9

SPIES AND OTHER CHALLENGES IN THE WAR ZONE

I was sitting in the first floor room of a FOB in Mosul with General Mustafa and a western NGO leader I'll call Bill, and things were getting tense.

We had commandeered the building for use during operations in that area. It was around eleven o'clock at night, and everyone was beat from a long day of work in the field. Now it was time to plan the next day, but unusually, two strangers were with us, both Europeans. One appeared to be Swedish, the other perhaps Eastern European. Mustafa sat there looking at them; before we began talking, he said, "I know everyone here but you. Who brought you in here?"

Bill said, "They're with me."

Mustafa's expression did not change. He stared at the guys and sized them up.

Good, I thought. I'd had a bad feeling about them since running across them a few days earlier. My rule in heightened scenarios is, don't move and groove with people you don't know. Beyond that, I just felt disquieted about them, as if they weren't being open about their identity and reason for being there. The look on Mustafa's face told me he was going to get to the bottom of who they were.

Bill continued, "This guy has been with me before, but I don't know this guy. He's his friend."

Yeah, not good. We had a guy in the room none of us knew. It wasn't just awkward; it was potentially dangerous. Mustafa's bodyguard subtly tapped the rifle slung around his chest. Bill's "friend" stood up.

"We're freelance journalists," he announced as if seizing the high ground. I sat back, enjoying the show and wondering how it could still be over ninety degrees near midnight. The building had no electricity—but it was more than heat making our guests sweat.

Through an interpreter, Mustafa demanded quietly, "Show me a website of your work."

This reasonable request flustered the Europeans. For a few minutes, they jabbered about their credentials, getting louder as they went. Not a good sign. I stood up to play Mustafa's wingman. I also wanted to speed things along so I could get to bed at some point.

"Listen, we don't know y'all, and I don't like the way you're talking," I said. "Give me both your IDs."

They blanched.

"I don't have to give you my ID," the Swede said.

"In your mind you don't think you have to, but you do," I said calmly.

He repeated, "I don't have to give you my ID."

This was interesting. "Look around," I said. "You don't get to make that decision here."

His eyes admitted defeat, and they both reluctantly pulled IDs from their pockets. I took photos of the cards and sent them to my intel guy right away. "Run these guys and let me know what you find," I texted him.

Mustafa had a sixth sense for infiltrators, and that instinct was on full display now.

"My team feels like you are ISIS," he said without a trace of emotion. Bill's eyes went wide, and so did those of his visitors.

Brave move, I thought, trying to make sense of it. The men did not fit the normal ISIS profile. Yes, there were foreign nationals, including Europeans, among ISIS, but to come right out and say it to someone took some guts, or maybe some intel I didn't know about.

"My guys want to kill you both," Mustafa continued, almost casually.

The Europeans' defensive patter had stopped. Clearly, it hadn't worked. The Swede was poking around on his phone, presumably to find evidence of his journalistic activity. Something boomed outside at a distance—the ongoing sounds of war, even at this hour. Mustafa looked at Bill as if to say, *I don't think you know these guys like you think you do.*

Muttering excuses, the Europeans failed to pull up any evidence that they were journalists.

"I … I can't get the sites to load," the Swede stuttered.

Silence. Mustafa glanced around with irritation. His guards shifted, their weapons clinking against their shirt buttons. Then the other guy—the total unknown—took out his phone and started typing rapidly. The interpreter didn't have to wait for a command from his boss. "Stop what you're doing," he demanded.

The guy foolishly kept typing. Sure, he might have been texting his wife that he was in a bad situation, but it looked a lot like he was trying to send out coordinates, or alert someone that he'd been caught, or destroy something on his phone before we could see it.

The interpreter repeated: "Stop what you're doing!"

A guard walked over and took the phones from both guys. Just then, my intel guy texted me back:

One guy is on an ISIS watchlist. The other is using a fake name.

How fun. I announced the findings to the room. Mustafa looked at the Europeans as if to give them a chance to respond. Bill sat there, gulping.

"That is not true!" the visitors said, turning up the volume again.

Mustafa looked at them, then at Bill. With no change of expression, he weighed the situation before him, then spoke.

"I'll give you a chance," he said, indicating with his eyes that it was only for Bill's sake. "You can't stay with us, so you have to leave. With no phones, nothing."

"Where do we go?" the Swede sputtered.

"That's not my problem," Mustafa said.

"We'll never make it out of here," said the other man.

Mustafa shook his head. Still not his problem.

That was it. The guards took the Europeans by the shoulders and marched them into the darkness outside. I can't prove it, and I didn't hear the gunshots, but I think Mustafa's men took them for a pleasant evening walk and then killed them both. We found out later they had been part of an ISIS intelligence-gathering cell.

It was one of many revelations about life in a combat zone. You could not predict what each day, or hour, would bring. No situation was ever what it seemed. You ran into bad actors and weird people from all around the world, some seeking excitement, some seeking a cause to live and die for, some seeking money.

In this case, the guys were seeking information that could have cost us our lives.

Pastor Disaster in Iraq

On other occasions, the problem was the guys we brought into the country.

Early on, I had the bright idea of bringing American pastors with us to Iraq to minister to people. I was sure it would create cross-cultural relationships and understanding between American Christians and Iraqi Christians, and maybe provide a pathway for American churches to support their beleaguered brethren overseas. Instead, the experiment turned into a huge headache and embarrassment for us. American pastors just did not know how to conduct themselves in a foreign place or a combat zone. Under pressure, every ounce of hidden cowardice or pride came oozing out of them.

One pastor told me halfway into the trip, "I really feel called to head back now. I feel like I've done what I was supposed to do."

He and I were sitting at a table together, and I became suddenly very perturbed.

"Really?" I said. "You want to go home right now?"

"Yeah," he said, "I think I accomplished what the Lord has for me here."

I loved the way he spiritualized it. But, as I say, courage is a requirement and quitters need not apply, so I surprised him by agreeing with him whole-heartedly—it was time for him to go home. I didn't want him there anymore.

"Good," I said, nodding. "Go back."

"What?" he blurted out, as if expecting me to try to dissuade him.

"I agree with you. You're done here," I said, and we made arrangements for him to leave as soon as possible.

Then I made the ill-advised decision to take some American pastors to speak to gatherings of persecuted Christians who had been attacked and harassed and whose churches had been bombed. One American guy stood up in front of them and said, "I oversee sixteen hundred churches in the United States and Canada." He went on boasting about the size and reach of his ministry, exalting himself before those faithful Iraqi pastors and their wives. It was as if he was going to tell them how to stay strong and bear up under persecution. It was ridiculous.

The next guy got up and did even worse. He started preaching some canned message. After a moment, an Iraqi pastor who I knew worked a full-time government job to support his ministry, and whose wife had terminal cancer, raised his hand and asked sweetly and deferentially, "Brother, can you please slow down? You are preaching too fast for us to understand."

This American buffoon puffed up and replied, "You'd better keep up, brother, because I'm preaching the Word of God."

The Iraqi pastor said, "I'm sorry."

I wanted to send the American pastor back to the States in a body cast. By the end of the trip, I was scheming about driving the whole group half-way to Mosul and dropping them off, just to see how influential and brave they were then. The worst part was, I knew they would go back home and strut around before their congregations like they had done a noble thing.

After my second batch of bad pastors, I swore I'd never do it again. And I'm glad I never have. Don't take clowns anywhere unless you want a circus.

Prayer Warrior

Then there were unexpected blessings. I'm thinking of Kelly Wilkerson, whose husband Gary leads the international ministry World Challenge. Kelly is an amazing woman of prayer, full of joy and as peaceful and gentle as you can imagine. Eileen and I knew her and Gary well, and we greatly admired both of them, but I was surprised when Eileen invited Kelly to go with us to Camp al-Hol in Syria, one of our more dangerous assignments.

It's alright. Kelly will just pray, hear the Lord about it and turn us down, I thought. But the opposite happened: Kelly called Eileen back and said, "I think I'm supposed to go with you to Syria."

Yikes. I couldn't shake my concern, so one night when we were having dinner at the Wilkersons' house, I pulled Gary aside.

"I know Kelly says she'll go to the Middle East with us, but do you know how dangerous this mission is?" I asked. "She literally could get really killed. I want to tell you, husband to husband, that this will be one of the most dangerous places we go."

I thought he would intervene and say, "Oh, wow, you're right. Let me talk her out of it," like most guys would.

Nope.

He smiled at me. "She prayed about it and says the Lord told her it was fine," he replied. "She'll go."

That was it. Not even a second thought. The Wilkersons were clearly either spiritual giants or very reckless people.

So Kelly was there for the crisis at the Syrian border with our vehicles and weapons. She was with us on the hot, treacherous highways of ungoverned Syria. With us at the nasty motel and in the camp full of ISIS families.

Through it all, she exhibited zero fear and zero apprehension. Her official task on the team was to pray because she has been an intercessor for a long time. Throughout that whole, challenge-filled experience, she sat serenely in the vehicle, quietly praying and radiating God's joy. I don't think I heard one word of concern from her the entire time.

When Eileen and I assessed the experience back home, we were convinced that we got through checkpoints and obstacles because Kelly was warring in the spirit for our team's success. We had no other explanation. Not only that, but Kelly conducted herself like a sacrificial traveler, never wincing or complaining at the many discomforts we endured to make it all work. She was our secret weapon; the reason we believe we made it all the way through to the ISIS camp and back.

Against the Violent Mob

Sometimes, in hectic situations, the people you're ministering to become, for a moment, your opponents.

One time we arrived at an IDP camp to give away toys, mittens, candy, and an assortment of supplies. The goodies van arrived before the security van did, and hardly had we turned off the motors and begun to unload give-aways than a wave of kids big and small came running toward us eagerly. They were there for the bounty, and there were a lot more of them than there were of us. Our security guys were nowhere in sight. Somehow, greedy pandemonium took hold, and the big kids began trampling the little kids, stepping on their heads, and seizing the stuff they wanted from us and from them. It was a devilish and horrible display, and someone easily could have been killed underfoot.

At that moment, a guy we didn't know who lived in the camp heard the screaming and came bolting out of his tent. He immediately grabbed a length of hose and began whipping the big kids on their bodies and backs. This broke the spell and caused some of the belligerent kids to run away from the van. Seeing that our rescuer needed help and that his solution was working, I ran over to him, grabbed another piece of hose, and joined him! The irony struck me immediately. Here I was, a global advocate for women and children, flailing teenagers with a hose—and, frankly, enjoying it because they were stepping all over the poor little ones and hurting their bodies. Maybe it was Iraqi Therapy; all I knew was I was defending little kids from violent big kids.

It worked. The big kids backed off, our security guys rolled up, and we decided to just get out of there before our presence caused anyone else to get hurt. Not everything goes according to plan.

Mental Battles

But the hardest things by far were the mental battles I fought before going on missions and after coming home. The whisper of the enemy when I geared up for trips was, "You're going to die. You're pushing too far." I had to stand on the fact that the Lord gave us those missions. I said, "Shut up, enemy. God called us to do this. If I die, I die."

Sometimes he went after me on the way home from a tough pump. One time, on a flight back from Iraq, my body suddenly started shaking, and I had trouble breathing. I couldn't stop reliving the recent experiences and thinking, *What on earth did we just do? How did we survive?*

"Chaz," I said, as the episode intensified, "go get Justin."

Justin was a former Green Beret on our team. He saw what was happening and sat next to me. He knew what to do.

"Victor, start talking to me right now," he said. "Start talking. Say everything that happened. Tell me everything you remember. Say it!"

Special ops guys know how to take people through those moments. I guess the mind compartmentalizes experiences, and then you get on a plane and the reality of what you just did crashes in on you.

That's why when people say, "It must be so great to do what you do," I want to tell them that the downsides are real and re-entry gets harder as I get older, not easier. Our team members struggle to sleep when we return. Bad dreams haunt us. Physical and emotional recovery takes a while.

One time, I was having a hard time thinking back on all the evil I'd seen in Mosul. I couldn't get my head together, so Eileen finally put me in a Jeep with Scout and said, "Take whatever weapons you want, drive to Oregon, and spend time with your friend out there. He'll know how to handle you. Stay gone as long as you need to."

I took that advice and did some shooting, climbed a glacier, jumped into an alpine lake, all that stuff. It was probably the closest I've come to tasting what true warriors feel when they return to "normal" society. Those mission-oriented, high-speed guys thrive on killing bad guys. They work sometimes in the kind of carnage you and I only see in video games. Imagine that your daily routine calls for hunting bad guys every night, hitting half a dozen houses or rooftops from a helicopter. You rush in, shoot the targets, capture who or what you need, and do it again the next night. Day in and day out, you perform at the highest level. In some cases, you're getting direct orders from the president filtered down through military bureaucracy.

It's hard to come back to a regular environment after that kind of lifestyle.

Other elite ops guys feel tremendous guilt for things they witnessed but did not do. Here's what I mean: When special operators are tracking weapons (and money), hunting bad guys, and gathering intelligence, they see the ugly side of criminal cartels and regimes. That means sex trafficking of the grossest sort—and the problem is that the special ops guys can't do anything about it because it's not part of their mission.

So imagine your ops team is surveilling a bad guy's house. You see a car pull up and an adult carrying or dragging two children into the house. Your team knows the bad guy himself is not there that night, but it's clear there will be harmful activity happening in his absence. If you pull the trigger now, you lose the opportunity to get your main target, but you potentially rescue children.

This happened to a friend, who begged his superiors to let the team go in and rescue the children. The response?

"Kids aren't our priority."

He finally convinced his chain of command to let his team go in to gather information; they found one child dead and one alive and being held in a closet.

That'll mess with your head.

I have experienced just a small portion of that. Maybe my hardest habit to shake has been the kind of hypervigilance that constantly asks, "Am I safe?" When we traveled regularly to Iraq, I would get back to our American home and hang a rifle and loaded magazines next to my bed. Yes, there were good reasons for this. I was resisting ISIS in a high-profile way and could expect retribution; but the Bible still says God hasn't given us a spirit of fear or an anxious mind, and sometimes the line between vigilance and paranoia became blurred.

It was hard to reacclimate to American consumer culture. Once, I went into a grocery store intending to pick up some cereal, but I stood there in the cereal aisle and found I couldn't make a decision. There were just too many boxes. I felt overwhelmed and sickened by the gluttony of it all. I had just been in a place where nothing is wasted, where people survive on flour and oil, and cheese when they can get it. The cost of a package of cereal alone, not to mention the marketing, shipping, and stocking of those rows of boxes, would have provided food for untold numbers of the kids we were reaching. I've never apologized for the blessings God has given America, but what are we using those abundant blessings for—our own comfort and pleasure only, or for others as well?

It's a dangerous question with, I think, a dangerous answer.

Think Tank "Experts"

Once, after coming back from the Middle East, I went to Washington, D.C., to speak at a luncheon about our recent trip. I was addressing a group of leaders from a well-known, highly regarded think tank which helped set policy direction for the United States, and they wanted to hear how ISIS was operating. I told them several things, including the fact that I had just met with an influential Muslim cleric who showed me an abandoned church that had belonged to persecuted Christians. Those Christians had fled the violence, and the church had become a makeshift shelter, with curtains hung to portion the space into separate "rooms." The whole place was terribly overcrowded with refugees.

The experience was fresh, and I related it from my heart.

Afterward, the leader of the think tank looked at me and said loudly, "I don't believe you."

I nodded.

"Okay," I said, and started eating my lunch.

Our ministry takes no money from public sources; we have God's favor on us to do His will, and I don't care who believes me. But those leaders were stunned by my response, and the table got quiet and awkward. The reason the man didn't believe me was that the particular Muslim leader I had referenced was very powerful in the Middle East, and not many Americans had met with him.

I'll never forget what happened next. The disbelieving guy mumbled a little louder than he probably intended, "But then again, I've never met with a senior Islamic leader. I've never even been to Iraq."

I could handle hearing the one thing but not the other. I put my fork down.

"You've never been to Iraq?" I said.

He shook his head—and I shook mine. It's amazing, the kind of people leading our country's foreign policy.

Christian Conference Confrontation

High on the list of unpleasant things I faced when coming home to the United States was Christian apathy—but that's how I met one of the great culture warriors of our day, Eric Metaxas.

I had made the mistake of flying directly from Iraq to the annual National Religious Broadcasters convention in Nashville, Tennessee. That meant I went from a violent, high-risk missionary assignment where I saw dead people, visited persecuted Christians, and tangled a bit with ISIS to a large convention center in a hotel the size of a small town with a bunch of well-fed American Christians hawking their ministries and radio shows. I had never attended an NRB convention before. My stateside team was going to meet me there, but for the first half-day I was by myself, without adult supervision, which turned out to be a less-than-optimal idea.

I walked into the big arena and instantly hated the vibe. It stank of insincerity and greed. Naturally, I gravitated to the security guys, the ones with earpieces who were practicing situational awareness. At least they weren't in on the racket. One guy sported a beard and his manner suggested he was the team lead. I took a chance and approached him.

"Hey, brother. How you doing?" I said, introducing myself. "I just got back from Mosul. I'm a high-risk missionary." At the time, that wasn't a strange way to start a conversation with someone in his industry because a lot of security contractors and special ops guys were going to work with the Iraqi government.

He grinned. Instant camaraderie. He was, indeed, the team lead.

"How you doing, man?" he asked.

"Good. It's weird being here," I told him. "I feel like flipping tables over more than anything."

"I'll tell you what," he agreed.

After chatting a moment, I talked with other security guys, eventually coming upon a row of booths for radio shows broadcasting in what looked like a large breezeway. One of the hosts was Eric Metaxas, whose books I was familiar with but whom I had never met. I resonated with his perspective. The first Christian book I ever read after coming to the Lord when I was in the Marine Corps was Dietrich Bonhoeffer's *The Cost of Discipleship*, and, of course, Eric wrote his definitive modern biography. *The Cost of Discipleship* blew up the "normal" modern Christian mold for me. I forever after embraced the idea of dying for my faith in service of what's right; building God's Kingdom, not my own; never making decisions based on comfort or convenience; always getting up after stumbling; and accepting no sin as part of my life, but always taking it openly and honestly to the foot of the Cross.

In front of Eric's broadcasting platform were thirty or so seats, so I sat down on the front row to listen. He happened to be interviewing a well-known religious leader about ISIS. This man was carrying on about the evils of Islam.

"Every Muslim is an extremist," the man said. "Their religion is tearing apart the world. They are the antithesis of love. They are the biggest threat to America."

The man had zero love for Muslims. Zero understanding of Muslim people's everyday lives and struggles. Zero perspective on what most Muslims thought about ISIS. On and on he went. At some point, the veins began popping out of my neck and I could barely contain myself. Eric took the show to a break, and he and the guy sat there talking off mic. Without any sensible person there to restrain me, I stood up, walked over, pulled an actual ISIS headband from my backpack, and slammed it on their table. (Let's just say I had gotten it from a guy who didn't need it anymore. It may have been warm when I acquired it, and it may even have been wet.)

The guest and the show's producer recognized what it was and seemed ready to soil their pants. The guest obviously thought I was ISIS-affiliated and had been sent to kill him. His face paled like a fainting woman's. The one guy who didn't flinch was Eric.

"No, I'm not ISIS," I said to them angrily and loudly. "No, I'm not an ISIS sympathizer."

I knew no one would haul me away because the security guys all knew who I was by then. I bet they were chuckling.

"I just got back from Iraq," I continued. "I'm one of the Christians out there trying to save lives. I'm seeing people butchered and I know what ISIS does to make Muslims extreme. I know the process."

I looked right at the minister, which was strange because I knew his face well from television, books, and magazines.

"You don't know what you're talking about, and worse than that, you're going to cause Muslims to *become* extreme because of what you're saying," I said.

I snatched the headband and walked away. I was so mad. That pastor was the epitome of a soft Christian who regurgitated stuff he'd heard, maybe from think tanks, and recycled it into sound bites that sounded cool to him and his audiences. Instead of creating any kind of sympathy or love for people trapped in that religion and those movements, he was telling Christian listeners to build a wall around their lives, their thoughts, and their churches that excluded "the least of these." It was like he wanted them to be blind and deaf to the cries of kids all over the world, to tune out their suffering. His foolish, inflammatory words might even have helped undo the good work our teams were doing.

Suddenly, I felt a hand on my shoulder. I turned and saw one of Eric's security team members.

"Who are you?" he asked.

"No one of consequence, but I do know the truth, and what that man was saying isn't it," I said. "He's going to cause a rise in extremism by feeding Christians absolute nonsense."

"What's your name?"

"Victor Marx," I said. "I just got back from Iraq. This is what I do."

"Can you wait here a second?" he said, and went back to Eric. A moment later he returned to me and said, "Eric wants to know if you'll be on his show for five minutes."

That was a surprise.

"Sure, but all I know how to do is tell the truth," I said.

"That's what he wants," Eric's guy said.

We walked over to the broadcasting platform. I met Eric properly, and he bumped another guest's slot to put me on.

"Folks, I've got to tell you. Something just happened that will blow your mind," Eric said in his own inimitable way. "I was talking to this other guest and this guy comes up and slams an ISIS headband down. Today we have Victor Marx. Did you just get back from Iraq? Tell us what that was about."

Five minutes turned into fifteen, and at one point Eric said, "I have literally never met anybody like you. You're blowing my mind."

"Do you want to see something else?" I offered, since he was egging me on. I pulled from my backpack a fourth-grade math workbook developed by ISIS. (Yes, ISIS developed their own curricula for kids.) One of the problems said something like, "If there are three hundred infidels and you have fifteen AKs, how many rounds would you need to shoot each infidel more than once?" As morbid as it was, their fourth-grade math problems were much harder than what American kids learn. I was shocked at the level of education ISIS delivered.

After we finished the interview, Eric said, "I want us to be friends."

I grinned. "Me, too," I said, and we kept our word.

But when I hopped off the platform to walk away, a group of men swarmed me and wanted to know about what I'd seen, if ISIS was as bad as they heard on the news, and what we could really do about them. I was heartened by their interest and their desire to hear the truth, not some religious caricature meant to sensationalize hatred for ministry gain.

Unbelievably, the guest I had confronted walked up to the circle of men and started to challenge me, interjecting his viewpoint into what I was saying. I was amazed. This guy had a national profile, had written books, and was on the radio, yet he needed to pick a fight with an unknown—me—in a breezeway at a convention. I finally turned to him and said, "Are you trying to aggravate me? Because you're getting pretty close to it."

I could feel the guys around me go, *Whoa.*

"No, I'm not intentionally trying to," the man said, backing off.

"Trust me, you don't have any idea what you're talking about with Muslims and radicalization," I assured him.

I guess what I'm saying is, when we strive to be the dangerous gentlemen we are made to be, we won't become more "normal" as the culture around us defines it, but less. God will give you life-changing experiences that radically shift your perspective on everything. What your life looks like from that point on depends on the kind of warrior you are meant to be.

And that's a great topic for the next chapter.

CHAPTER 10

WHAT KIND OF WARRIOR ARE YOU?

Chuck Holton, a former war correspondent for CNN and an Army Ranger, wrote a great book in which he said that Christians need to identify what kind of warrior they are. You see, not all warriors are the same. We would be weaker if we were. Even in a professional army there are frontline guys, rear echelon guys, supply line workers, cooks, corpsmen, generals, and privates. Each one has a different skill and a different experience of the war, though all are fighting for the same cause.

What is your place on the battlefield? In what way are you supposed to be a dangerous gentleman? Please don't wimp out and default to the easiest thing you can think of. Don't just make it about justifying your present circumstance. Ask God, "Where should I stand, even at risk of losing things that are precious to me? Who can I defend? Who can I help save? Where can I give my life for You?"

"I Am a Warrior"

There are, of course, Dave Eubank-types of dangerous gentlemen. These guys are rare. They live in jungles without reliable sources of water and food, without the luxuries of modern plumbing, flushable toilets, and nearby coffee shops. They may live and serve and raise their kids in active civil war zones.

We've all heard about missionaries who gave their lives in places like China, Africa, India, and South America. While not every Christian man is called to be a Dave Eubank, a Hudson Taylor, or a Jim Elliott, the courage and self-denial they and their families embody should describe each of us, wherever we are called to serve. If you're curious whether you are a closet Eubank, just ask God about it. Maybe the answer will radically change your life.

I am a different kind of warrior than that. I was raised in violence, and God also gave me natural abilities as a fighter. Both those things prepared me for a career in the martial arts and training thousands of people in the use of firearms, blades, and bare hands (and feet). God also made me to serve in full-time ministry assignments. So I have a strange combination of ministry grace and an innate sense of how to move and groove in combat situations. I think God uses my life, in part, to highlight a certain mindset Christians will need in the days to come. What I know for sure is that I feel weak in many areas of life, and every area of "strength" is a manifestation of God's grace. I also know that every person has a unique set of skills springing from their identity and calling in Christ.

I also know that, compared to professional warriors, my combat skills are really small. I know many individuals who are paid to kill bad guys, storm buildings, defend strategic military positions, and protect important people. I know one individual who has personally killed more than a thousand enemy fighters. Guys like that know how to win battles and conduct themselves in the meat grinder. Most people, including me, aren't built for that—but we need those guys, and they give us a vivid picture of what battle looks like in the physical realm.

One Delta operator and I were shooting steel targets in the Pacific Northwest one day. My shots sounded like, *Bing! ... Bing! ... Bing!* I was pleased to see the targets dropping one by one. Then the Delta operator said,

"Let me try." He stepped up, and his targets went, *Bing-bing-bingbingbing!* He nailed them all in a fraction of the time it took me.

"That's why you're Delta," I said, feeling three feet tall and severely humbled.

But later, when we were hanging out, that guy told me something surprising. He said, "You all are really cowboying out there in the Middle East. I have so much respect for that."

I thought he was mocking me, because he was the Delta operator and I ran a small ministry doing shoestring, pinpoint operations.

"Why would you say that?" I asked. He looked me straight in the eye.

"I've never been in a fair fight," he said. "We never face a foe worthy of what our force brings to the field. None of our enemies really stands a chance."

That really caught me. The United States overpowers its opponents with technology, training, and sheer tonnage. It's like a professional sports team playing the local rec league champions. The outcome is never in doubt. By comparison, our ministry teams lack anything like that level of muscle. We scrape together manpower and firepower to go unaided and with no backup into some of the riskiest neighborhoods on Earth. Somehow, God has allowed us to minister effectively and survive.

Again, different kinds of warriors, different battlefields. Both are necessary.

Everyone reading this book is called to stand in an important place, but in different settings. Some of you work for Fortune 500 companies, governments, or school districts where your values and beliefs are not just under fire but forbidden. The truth is, people on the home front—in civic life, workplaces, churches, schools and families—may face greater danger than Delta guys do. Because unlike you or me, those well-paid, well-trained warriors will probably never end up in David-versus-Goliath situations where they could lose jobs, paychecks, houses, relationships, or reputations for standing for righteousness. Yet God calls everyday warriors to take those risks all the time.

I like what the prophet Joel said in the Bible. It's how I know each of us is some type of warrior:

> Proclaim this among the nations:
> Consecrate for war;
>   stir up the mighty men.
> Let all the men of war draw near;
>   let them come up.
> Beat your plowshares into swords,
>   and your pruning hooks into spears;
>   let the weak say, "I am a warrior." (Joel 3:9–10)

First, we have to understand that when it's time for war, you go to war, and when it's time for peace, you cultivate peace. The writer of Ecclesiastes tells us there are times for both. It's useless to proclaim peace when it's time for war, or war when it's time for peace. Moses called God Himself a "man of war" (Exodus 15:3), and according to the prophet Isaiah:

> The Lord goes out like a mighty man,
>   like a man of war he stirs up his zeal;
> he cries out, he shouts aloud,
>   he shows himself mighty against his foes.
> For a long time I have held my peace;
>   I have kept still and restrained myself;
> now I will cry out like a woman in labor;
>   I will gasp and pant.
> I will lay waste mountains and hills,
>   and dry up all their vegetation;
> I will turn the rivers into islands,
>   and dry up the pools. (Isaiah 42:13–15)

The passage from Joel gives hope to every man among us. He says not only should the "men of war" present themselves ready for battle, but "the weak" are commanded to announce, "I am a warrior."

Say that out loud: "I am a warrior."

I've had to do that thousands of times when fighting mental battles or overcoming obstacles or threats abroad or at home. Whenever I feel weak, I say, "I am a warrior," or something like it. I speak God's truth about myself until I feel confident about it, which the Bible calls faith. You can do the same thing. In fact, we must declare, "I am a warrior," when it's time for war.

Assassin's Gift

I met a guy once whom I guess you would call a mercenary, though I don't like that term. Like so many in his trade, he felt he was going through life alone. Many guys in military and paramilitary professions have a hard time keeping long-term relationships and marriages going. They are loners by profession, but they are still humans and they long for deep friendships. Some are addicted to everything from alcohol to cold medicine—I've seen it all. Many have trouble sleeping. Many have a hard time seeing any good in the world.

My conversation with that guy was infused with the presence of the Holy Spirit, and he was really receptive to the revelation of God's love. He was so moved that, as a gesture of thanks, he pulled out an important possession: his assault knife. It's not really called an "assault knife" but that's what it's for. It was a primary tool of his job, and therefore a priceless possession.

"Here," he said. "I want you to have this."

He set the well-used blade in my hand as a token of sincere gratitude. I couldn't believe he was giving it to me.

"Thank you," I said. "I receive this and everything it means."

As we parted ways, he said rather hesitantly, "That knife—you may need to clean it off. There might be some blood on it."

He didn't mean his own blood, I assure you. Are there really warriors like that in the world? Yes, and they need ministry as much as you and I do. In fact, they deal with issues that touch life and death all the time. They can suffer from a sense of guilt—or worse, a lack of guilt, which tends to bother them more. Some are essentially stuck in their careers as assassins because it doesn't have many transferable skills. Some only feel alive with the challenge and focus combat offers.

In another country, I met a gentle, kind man who had killed more than twenty people in close combat with a knife while serving as a bodyguard for a royal family. I taught him some advanced blade work and gave him my Marine Corps KA-BAR knife as a gift. Over a meal in the jungle, I asked him, "What's your biggest takeaway from having to kill all those guys with your blade?"

He thought for a moment, then replied, "Some die quick, some die slow," and kept eating. He had distilled it down to that and didn't seem bothered by it. When I got back home, I received a video message from the guy saying, "May God bless you, and thank you so much for the knife you gave me."

I bring these things up because, in the West, we've been so insulated from violence and danger that we don't realize that the world is full of both. We find those realities revolting or shocking. That's fine, but the existence of people who deal in high-risk protection and safety should at least get us thinking: If we're not that kind of warrior, what kind are we? Are we putting our lives on the line like they are?

In what way are we being dangerous gentlemen in our own circumstances?

Other Types of Power

I've met many different people operating as warriors in their own spheres around the globe. I think of a Muslim cleric who has become my good friend. He stood up to ISIS in a big way, religiously and intellectually, and they drove him out of his city and took all his belongings, leaving him poor but still highly regarded by Muslims worldwide. One day, he took my team to a church from which Christians had fled. We walked in. It was in a horrible condition, destroyed and desecrated—and full of a new wave of refugees, many of them Christians.

The cleric turned to me and said, "These persecuted Christians are your people. Where are the American Christians?"

The question caught me flat-footed. All I could say in response was, "They're afraid of death. That's why they're not here."

He smiled with puzzled curiosity and said, "But we all die."

That man was fighting his battles mostly through sermons and lectures—but he had every bit as much courage as a frontline soldier. His life was literally on the line, and he could have been assassinated at any time.

Once, in a very high-security setting, he scooted close to me and said, "I'd like to tell you something." In a hushed tone, so that nobody could even read his lips, he continued, "Would you like to know where an ISIS training camp is?"

I was taken aback. That was very valuable information.

"Sir, if you give me that information, what would you want me to do with it?" I asked.

He said very practically, without vengeance or anger, "Kill them. Kill them all."

Like me, he wanted to help stop the ISIS death machine, to save innocent lives from their merciless hands.

"I have friends who are very good at doing that," I said.

He smiled. "I knew you could do something," he said.

Mo's Story

One time I met an Iraqi named Mo. His Shia Muslim family had been persecuted and killed under Saddam Hussein's Sunni Muslim regime, and sixteen-year-old Mo had fled to a refugee camp in Saudi Arabia. A more accurate term for that is "prison camp," because it had towers and guards with guns, and they shot you if you tried to leave. After a couple of years seeing people die there, Mo obtained a visa to go to America. But once he arrived, he had no money, so he just wandered the streets.

"Do you know who helped me, Victor?" he told me. "A Christian church. I went there and they helped me. For that, I'm forever grateful to Christians."

He married a Christian girl and gained United States citizenship. When terrorists attacked America on September 11, 2001, he enlisted in the US Army and became an intelligence gatherer for Special Forces units in Iraq. They made him an interpreter and called him "the Bear" because he is barrel-chested like a wrestler and has freakish strength. He could grab a guy and put him through a wall. Mo is all courage in many ways.

Of all the cool stuff Mo has done, "orphanage founder" tops his list. I consider him a perfect example of a dangerous gentleman. He's physically huge and unusually strong. He's also brilliant. But more than anything, his heart beats to bring justice and protection to the weak. He could be pulling down big money in any number of jobs here in the United States—owning a nice house, buying cars, taking vacations, and racking up retirement money. But Mo puts himself in harm's way to defend kids and help vulnerable people.

That example challenges us to do the same, wherever we are.

The Friendly Interrogator

Buddy is on my board of directors, and he is considered perhaps the best interrogator of terrorists our country has had in recent decades. Buddy has performed more than three thousand interrogations for United States military and civilian law enforcement agencies, and he became famous for flipping people from being terrorists to helping stop terrorists. That's a big deal.

Why were bad guys willing to switch sides? Because Buddy is one of the nicest people you will ever meet. He is genuine, sincere, likable, and fun. He is a relational interrogator; he builds trust with people and never betrays it.

Typically, Buddy tells a detainee, "I'm part of the intel group here and I really need to get some information from you, but I will never lie to you. I'm not going to manipulate you. That's just not how I do it."

Sometimes he goes further and says, "I'm going to stay with you in your cell for three days. You'll have the opportunity to kill me because we'll be sleeping in the same cell, but it won't turn out good for you, so my recommendation is, don't try."

While living with a suspect, Buddy gets to know about the guy's family, the tribal issues back home, the things that are important to him. People come to trust him. One time Buddy told me, "When they lied to me, it was easy to know because they'd told me the truth so many times."

Buddy built actual relationships with people. If one of the prisoner's family members died on the outside, Buddy grieved and asked how he could help. He sometimes even visited those families.

Buddy's weapon is integrity. He tells people all the time that integrity is one of the greatest assets anyone can have. Now, when people join our team, they have to be interviewed by Buddy. When my daughters get serious about a guy, I not only run background checks but have the guy talk to Buddy. Buddy asks the same question ten different ways with ten different intonations, looking for inconsistencies, motivations, and sincerity. My middle daughter has a husband today because he passed the Buddy test.

Buddy's not a battlefield guy, but his work is hugely effective. He's a dangerous gentleman in his own powerful way.

Boldly Spiritual

Some dangerous gentlemen are built for spiritual battlefields. I met such a guy at my house one day, and he took such a risk with me that I nearly clobbered him and threw him off my deck.

It happened around the time God was shifting us toward the Middle East. I needed a fence installed, so I called a guy I had never met for a bid. He arrived, we shook hands, and I told him what we wanted. He took his equipment out and walked the property. When he was done, he knocked on the sliding glass door of our deck, and I joined him outside.

"Can I ask why you want this fence?" he asked.

"Yeah, I do stuff overseas that requires some security here," I said.

"What do you do?" he asked.

"Ministry, humanitarian work," I said.

He nodded as if he'd sort of expected that.

"I used to travel in South America as an evangelist and do crusades," he said. "Tens of thousands of people came to faith through our meetings."

"Really? Why'd you stop?" I asked.

"The Lord told me to come home and raise my boys," he said. "Let me ask you something. Do you want all the gifts God wants for you?"

This was an abrupt question, but I could sense the authority of God in his voice.

"What'd you say?" I asked, to make sure I'd heard him right.

"Do you want all God has for you in the area of gifts?" he said—meaning spiritual gifts. He was completely no-nonsense.

"Hang on a second and let me think," I said.

This was potentially a big deal. I know God well enough to understand that you don't just get gifts without responsibility—and I felt full-up with responsibilities right then. As I considered it, the fence maker stood there watching me, like, *Make up your mind, man.*

So I prayed, *Lord, if this is real, will You give me the grace to handle whatever goes with it?*

I felt the Spirit's confirmation, so I said, "Yeah, okay. I do want all God has for me in the area of gifts."

"Great. I'll pray for you," the man said, stepping toward me.

"Hold on," I said. "Let me get my wife."

I opened the sliding door. Eileen was in the living room.

"Hey, honey, this guy's going to pray for me," I said. "I don't know who he is or if he's weird, but I want a witness if I have to throw him off the balcony."

"Okay," she said, as if I'd told her I was watering the lawn. She stepped out and joined us.

"Let's hold hands," the man said.

Agh! He's a hand-holder, I thought. Not my favorite thing.

He closed his eyes and began praying. I always keep my eyes open when praying. I look around shamelessly. (Don't judge.) The guy went right into shouldaboughtaHyundaibutIboughtaKia, praying in tongues, which was fine with me.

"Lord, impart to this man all the gifts that he needs!" he said, and pulled my hand toward him. When I pulled back, he turned and punched me full-on in the stomach—and never stopped praying! He didn't even open his eyes when he threw the fist. My hackles went straight up. Eileen looked at me like, *Uh-oh, what is my husband going to do?*

Heedless of danger, the guy kept praying, "Holy Ghost, fill him! Give him all he needs!"

Then he punched me a second time! *Hard.* In nanoseconds I thought, *Is this guy nuts? He just punched me twice. What do I do? Knock him out? Throw him overboard? Because he's fully nuts.* In the same nanosecond I prayed, *Lord, is this You? If I resist getting hit, is that rebellion? Can I tighten my stomach up or should I relax if he hits me again? I don't know how this spiritual stuff works.*

I noticed that Eileen hadn't broken away or told the guy, "Hey, knock it off." She stayed in the moment, so I tried to as well.

I almost couldn't believe it when Fence-Maker Man turned and hit me a third time. Nobody has ever done that without enjoying a response. Then he finished praying, opened his eyes, let go of our hands and said, "That's it." He started to walk away as if he were going home.

"Hey, sir," I called out. "Can we talk about this for a minute?"

"Sure."

He came back over.

"No one has ever punched me and not paid some type of price," I said.

"Yeah. It's weird, isn't it?" he said.

"You're right. It's weird," I agreed, but he didn't seem frightened by me. I was impressed by that.

"I come from a lineage of this stuff," he said. "I trained under Lester

Sumrall. I was on staff with him and traveled with him. Smith Wigglesworth is in my lineage, too."

Mr. Fence-Maker had no way of knowing that when I was in high school, I had gone to see Lester Sumrall speak at Rutgers University in New Jersey. I sat in the stands of some sports arena listening to him and thought, *God's hand is really on this guy. It's unmistakable. That's a true preacher. He speaks with the authority of God.* Decades later, one of his team members was punching me on my own deck.

"What's next?" I asked him. "What am I supposed to do?"

"Nothing," he said. "Just watch and see what happens. Apparently, I wasn't here for the fence."

That was it. He turned and walked away, never gave me a bid, never spoke with me again. But whatever he did, it worked. After that, I developed a radical boldness when speaking to audiences. This power came on me and never left, and I knew it was because of that bizarre encounter.

I tell that story because that guy was another kind of warrior—a weird one, but very effective in his own way. He was willing to do things I don't think I would ever do. He had no fear of me. He didn't want my money or anything. He just wanted to faithfully carry out the assignment God gave him that day—even if it got him pummeled.

Whatever we are called to do, that should be our attitude, too. Fearless and unashamed.

Old Man Strength

Some people think they are too old to be dangerous gentlemen or operate like warriors. I'm here to tell you there's no such thing as being too old. Moses, Joshua, and Caleb in the Bible had their most productive years after age eighty. Young guys may have excess energy, but old guys have determination and mental toughness. I like what people call it: "old man strength."

There's a funny saying in the military: Beware of an older man in a younger man's profession. Why? Because those guys are still around for a reason: They know what they're doing. They can defeat a young, brash dude with strategy and timing. I learned the importance of this from my dad. He taught me (mostly by kicking my butt around a dojo) that timing is different than speed. Speed is when I jump out of the way of a moving truck. Timing is when I saw it coming twenty seconds before it arrived and stepped back before it got close. In the ring, speed is my ability to punch or kick without my opponent detecting the blow before it lands. Timing is the ability to deliver a punch or kick the opponent moves into because he *never* saw it coming.

When my dad was in his fifties, a couple of world-class fighters came into my dojo to train in traditional karate. My dad watched them for a while, then took his shoes off and asked, "Can I work in a few rounds and be a body for y'all?" The guys didn't know who he was, and probably thought they'd have to go easy on him.

"Sure, come on in," they said.

They took turns sparring with him but couldn't land a punch. They ramped up the speed and started throwing harder, but my dad anticipated the punches and evaded them all. Not only that, but he countered with his own and began drilling these guys with impeccable timing. They were faster and stronger, but his timing was out of sight. They finally got so angry that they left.

When you master timing, you mess up people's rhythms and freak them out. Let's say I throw three jabs with my lead hand to your face. When I throw them, a predictable timing pattern would be, "One and two and three." Each time you would be able to block the punch because you knew it was coming. But if I changed the timing to, "One and two-three," now you'd probably get hurt and disoriented—and just like that, I'm on top of you. That's how quickly you can gain an advantage. Add blades or guns to the mix, and effective timing becomes deadly.

My point is that as we grow older, we gain more than we lose. Moses gained mercy and humility. Joshua grew in wisdom and courage. Caleb displayed as much fire at eighty as he did at forty. Yes, younger guys have quicker footwork, greater strength, and more flexibility, but "old master gladiators" (as my dad called them) have a lifetime of strategy and observation to draw on. They can predict what their opponent will do, and when they figure you out, they wipe the floor with you.

No matter your age, you have a place on the battlefield to which God has called you. Let the weak say, "I am a warrior." Dangerous gentlemen never give up and never retire. We keep going till the day we die.

One of my great inspirations in the long game is Nicky Cruz, who was a New York City streetfighter before his famous conversion to Christ, which is recounted in the classic book *The Cross and the Switchblade*. Eileen and I met Nicky at a health club in Colorado Springs right when I was starting to work in youth prisons. He was sixty-three, and I was impressed because he still consistently worked out.

"I'm resigning my position and starting a ministry of evangelism to young people in prisons," I told him.

He looked at me sincerely and said, "That's great. There are so few real evangelists anymore in the United States because the church does not encourage true evangelists."

We talked for a while and then he prayed for us, laying hands on us and saying, "Lord, give them the mind of Christ." Eileen and I both began crying because of the force of his words and the powerful presence of the Holy Spirit in that moment. It became a marker for us in ministry.

Nicky had "old man strength" in the realm of spiritual authority. By then, he had served in evangelistic ministry for more than forty years. There is no substitute for a long, faithful walk with Jesus. The power someone like that carries is beyond what any younger person has gained. Sometimes, to be dangerous in big ways, you have to be old.

Twenty years later, I ministered with Nicky in Cuba and felt like I was walking out the impartation he had given me at the gym that day. He was in his eighties then and still walked four miles a day. He was buoyant in spirit, always laughing and teasing people. He was so relaxed that it disarmed them.

Over dinner one night, I opened my heart to him and said, "I've been concerned because I feel like I'm getting older, and I see my limitations on some things. Darts of the enemy hit my mind and tell me I won't be used as much as I was before. I've been struggling with that."

Nicky leaned back and howled with laughter. All I could do was watch him.

"Victor!" he said. "Victor, look at me." He gestured to himself to indicate his age.

"I know, brother. I know," I said, smiling along with him. He laughed again, and it broke the power of those mental darts. I felt like my youth was renewed seeing a man in his eighties still ministering so effectively around the world.

I asked, "Nicky, what's the one piece of advice you can give that would help me?"

He responded almost immediately, "Beware the little foxes."

I sat there waiting for him to expound on it. He didn't, but the Holy Spirit did, and I knew he meant the whispers of the enemy in my mind. Since then, I have exercised greater discipline than ever in taking every thought captive. When the enemy comes at me with sweet-sounding doubts, I say, "I don't even have time for you. Get away from me." That's what Nicky taught me with his old man strength.

Dangerous gentlemen can look a thousand different ways and have a million different assignments, but all have courage, discipline, humility, selflessness, and the attributes of the Christian life described in the Bible. These are what make us strong, so when we head into the specific assignments the Lord gives us, we will always go forward in triumph no matter how old or young we are, or where we are called to be dangerous gentlemen.

CHAPTER 11

FIGHTING THE GOOD FIGHT

L et me share the best practical tips I have for those determined to be dangerous gentlemen. These things have helped me tremendously and are foundation stones in my life.

Be a Dad

The best thing any man can do for his family, society, and the Kingdom of
God is to fully embrace his role and responsibility as a father. This goes for
married guys and single guys, young guys, and old guys, because every guy
is a role model to somebody, even just by example. Being an older brother,
a mentor, an uncle, pastor, or boss all falls into the category of "fathering."

The family structure is breaking down in society generally—and in
Christian families as well. Too few dads exercise strong, humble, righteous
authority. It's like they're afraid they'll get in trouble with somebody if they
act like a dad. But when men step back and stop expressing fatherly authority and love, kids rebel against all authority. When a teacher, boss, or police
officer contradicts or instructs them, they don't know how to handle it. They
perceive authority as violent and controlling. It makes them feel "uncom-
fortable" and "unsafe." They grow up to be out-of-control adults because

they've never been taught to govern themselves and submit to something outside their own personal impulses.

Fatherlessness is the biggest problem in America and has led to a host of evils. Men should have stood up and said, "No way are we killing off the next generation," and stopped abortion from becoming legalized. The sexualization of public schools, the promotion of deviant lifestyles, and the charade of same-sex "marriage" all could have been stopped if men had acted like dangerous gentlemen in legislatures, courts, and schools. We have turned into a nation of impotent cowards instead of dangerous gentlemen—and we're reaping the results.

When a man exercises righteous authority in a gentle, firm, loving, consistent way, people come to trust him. They see that what initially made them feel "unsafe" is actually the safest thing in society. When people know that men are dangerous and gentle, they relax. They treat others with more respect. All the stats show that crime is lower in places where citizens are allowed to carry firearms in public and where families are more often intact. The population is safer because fewer bad guys are willing to take the risk of violating someone there. We've all seen surveillance videos of ex-Marines or old guys with guns firing a few rounds at a robber as the dude stumbles over himself to flee the scene. That's good stuff. That's dangerous gentlemen keeping society safe.

When everyone buys into that righteous standard, they start promoting it generally. They demand that others treat men—and women and children— with respect. They view manly authority as stabilizing, not controlling. They even insist that we men be the dangerous gentleman we were born to be. Remember when kids on the playground would brag about their dads? "My dad's better than your dad." Men in their proper place are a young person's dream come true. Kids want to boast about us for being strong and defending them, for guiding them, for caring about them.

Fatherly authority heals societies, families, and individual hearts. Be the dad and the man you were called to be. That's step one.

Stay Under Authority

As you grow into that role, stay under the authority of God.

All true dangerous gentlemen operate under God's authority. Period. There is no exception. Mavericks give dangerous gentlemen a bad name. None of us are called to be unaccountable despots in our families, businesses, churches, and so on. Thankfully, we have a picture of what operating under authority looks like. Jesus modeled submission to authority perfectly—always and *only* saying and doing things His Father led him to do. Families and societies will only submit to fatherly authority when they see that men are submitted to God. They want the security of knowing, "My dad (or mentor, boss, etc.) hears from God as best as he can, and he has no other motivation than to implement God's will for us."

That means a man must lead from his knees. This has to be done in some measure in his family's (or church's, or employees') presence. It may mean regularly gathering to fellowship and pray together. Your wife, kids, and subordinates need to hear you pray aloud. They have to see that God is the real boss. They must see you submitting to authority before they will submit themselves to *your* authority.

Some of you guys need to apologize to your family or church or whatever for not leading prayerfully sooner, then pledge to start giving better leadership and guidance from this day forward. That'll get their attention.

Stay on Assignment

If you've heard me speak recently, you know I often travel with the world's most awesome dog, Scout. She's a four-legged, ultrasmart biological weapon I can aim at anyone at any time with a word. Scout has no fear, as best I can tell.

Scout, although a female, exemplifies the best characteristics of a gentleman, and that's the part that amazes people. She's not just a hurt package on a leash; she is very gentle. We perform demonstrations in which she attacks one of my employees (how would you like that to be in your job description?) who wears a padded arm cover. It's a real attack; Scout doesn't know how to pretend. But when I call her off, the attack ends and then I do something even more surprising: I walk over to my employee, shake his hand and we walk away together, with Scout meekly by my side. Scout is not confused by this. She is as gentle as a lamb when commanded to be. She reminds me of Jesus: fierce and violent when needed, gentle at all other times. No wonder He is called "the Lion and the Lamb."

My point is this: Scout is always on assignment. Wherever I go, her eyes never leave me. In fact, the only time she spazzes out is in those infrequent situations when she doesn't have a task and doesn't know what she's supposed to do.

Like Scout, we need to keep our eyes on the Lord and stay on assignment. When we stay in His will, we can know for certain that we are safe and effective. All God requires is that we run in the lane He puts us in. We don't have to make stuff up.

I've seen guys in battle zones leave their assignments so they could find action elsewhere. I've also seen them limp back to camp in armored vehicles that had tires and windows blown out because they left the safety of their assignment. I'm zero impressed when guys nearly lose their lives because they went beyond their task. I've actually sent guys home for thrill-seeking. I tell them, "Don't come back. That's it. You're off the team."

To be a dangerous gentleman, you can't get offtrack. Distractions are everywhere, but we must remain focused.

Stay Hungry

All Things Possible held its first men's conference at an army base instead of a church some years ago, and there was a snowstorm that weekend. Both elements—the unusual location and the bad weather—worked against high attendance, but believe it or not, that's exactly what we wanted. We don't like feeding what we call "the fat guys"—those American Christian dudes who have all the teaching they need but never seem to do much with it. Having our conference at an army base during a snowstorm, and requiring registration and payment, filtered out those who didn't have the drive to put into practice what we gave them. We want men who are hungry, not full.

Half of the 130 men flew or drove in from around the country. One guy drove eight hundred miles to attend. But it was the Arab guy sitting in the audience wearing a typical Arab scarf that my team noticed right away. Because of our work against ISIS, we are always on the lookout for potential threats—guys who seem unusual, don't fit in, or have bulging jackets.

Between sessions, the Arab guy approached me, smiling. No bulging jacket, no obvious weapon, but our guys were on alert.

"Do you remember me?" he asked.

I looked at him closely, realizing I did recognize him.

"No way," I said. I shook his hand warmly.

"Yes, I flew here to hear you again," he said, grinning.

Rewind six years. I was speaking at a men's event in Missouri, and a guy with an Arabic name from the Pacific Northwest registered. My team ran his name and found he originally was from a certain Middle Eastern country.

"Just make sure your detail is aware of him," I told the event organizers.

Halfway through one of my messages, that guy stood up and walked out of the auditorium. Sheriff's deputies watched him go out the back door and sit in his car. They got a little nervous. After I finished my message, they told me, "The Arab guy wants to come back in, but we stopped him because he's getting irate. He's saying, 'I must see him. I must see Victor Marx. I can't talk to anyone else.'"

"Okay," I said, then prayed, "Lord, what do You want me to do?"

Green light. "Bring him to me," I told the security guys.

They brought him backstage, and as soon as he came in, he said, "You must pray for me. I have demons."

"Okay. Have a seat. Let's crush 'em," I said.

Three cops were standing in the adjacent hallway—one with his gun drawn—but the Arab guy wasn't packing anything, so I had them stand down. I prayed for the man, and he got free of demonic oppression. He stood up beaming, hugged me, and left.

"Lord, what was that about?" I asked when he was gone.

The Lord's answer was so clear: "That man had the faith to fly across the country to have you pray for him. His faith got him free."

Now, six years later, at our snowstorm event, the same guy had showed up. He told me he was an aerospace engineer who, since our previous encounter, felt called to minister to people in the Middle East and North Africa. He ended up becoming a supporter of our ministry.

That guy's hunger reminded me of people in the Bible who were so desperate for answers that they did extraordinary things. Hungry people make warrior moves. They are violent toward their own apathy, violent toward their critical lack, even violent toward their reputations and pocketbooks because freedom always costs you something.

Are you so hungry for what God has for you that you will give up normal comforts, cash, and convenience to grab it? What level of faith have you exercised to get an answer from God? That Arab guy was hungry and dangerous, and his faith still provokes me.

Hate the Right Things

We also have to hate some things to be dangerous gentlemen. First off, we have to hate sin. The Bible is super clear on this point. We can't just be annoyed by sin; we must hate it, detest it, have no taste for it, reject it out of hand. If we are not ready to do that, then we are not ready to follow the King. We must maintain an uncompromising attitude toward bad behavior and wrong heart attitudes. It is nonnegotiable.

I had a crazy experience one time in Birmingham, Alabama. Let me preface the story by saying that I am one of those guys that gets hit on by women when I travel. I don't like it, but it's a fact. The enemy hunts me down and puts the wrong people in my way. Eileen and I are fully aware of this and vigilant about it.

But in Birmingham that time, I felt that a bigger attack was underway, so I called Eileen.

"Something's up, babe," I told her. "I feel like there's a spirit of lust after me, and it's beyond normal. I know normal and I know weird—this is weird. Would you and the kids please pray for me?"

"Yeah, I'll get the kids right now," she said, and they did as I requested.

I was driving back to my hotel when a carload of college girls pulled up next to me and started hooting and hollering. I slowed down to get rid of them, but they slowed down to stay next to me. I sped up, so they sped up. Then one girl pulled her shirt up and I saw what only her child, her husband, and her doctor ought to see. The others were laughing and making nasty gestures to me.

Waiting desperately for the stoplight to turn green, I held up my left hand, pointed at my wedding ring and shouted with authority, "I'm married!" That had a real effect. They freaked out and sped off.

So far, so good. I parked at the hotel, still rattled by that strange encounter, and got into the elevator. But while the doors were shutting, a hand stuck in and the person reopened it. A nicely dressed woman in her thirties stepped in and smiled at me. I have a rule that I don't ride in elevators with women, but I didn't get out in time, so I was stuck. I was holding a box of ministry resources and considering using it as a shield, if necessary.

While the elevator was moving, she turned to me and said, "Can I get off on your floor?"

Ding! The doors opened, and my floor was first. I stepped quickly out and held the door with my foot while addressing her.

"Ma'am, I am not what you need," I said. "I can tell you're hurting but some romp with a stranger will not fulfill the need in your heart."

Then I handed her the box of resources and said, "You should take these." It served as a barrier and gave me time to run. I was concerned she would come after me and learn where my room was. Instead, she instantly dropped her head and said, "I'm a Christian and I'm going through a divorce. You're right. I'm hurting and I'm sorry for coming onto you like that."

I felt the heart of God in that moment and said, "God loves you so much that He put me here now to stop you from doing something stupid."

The doors shut. I waited a moment to make sure the elevator was gone, then bolted to my room and double-locked the door. (That woman ended up writing a letter to Focus on the Family to thank me for saving her from making a tragic mistake.)

I had survived the attacks so far, but they kept coming. I was packing my bags the next morning when the housekeeper knocked on the door.

"Can I start cleaning?" she asked.

"Yeah, I'm getting out of here," I said, and began to hustle to get out the door.

Instead, she said in a polite way, "Hey, you want to get together?" She meant right there in the room she was supposed to be cleaning.

"Look here," I said back to her, just as directly. "Has anyone ever shared the Gospel of Jesus Christ with you?"

"No," she said.

"May I?" I asked.

"Yeah," she said.

In that room with the door open, she listened to me and gave her heart to the Lord. She had never heard the Gospel and didn't know why Jesus came to Earth. I was certain that my wife and kids at home praying had a lot to do with the softness of her heart.

I made it out of the hotel safely, but the enemy wasn't done. On my way to the airport, I pulled over to gas up the rental car. There was a hooker going from car to car.

"Hey, what time's your flight?" she asked me. "You want me to help you with something?"

"Hold it right there," I said, putting up a hand. I still had some ministry resources in a box.

"Here," I said, handing her the box. "Sell these, make some money. My daddy used to run women. I understand your plight. All I can say is, the Lord is your only hope."

Then I got in the car and got out of there.

Here's how stupid and desperate the enemy was during that trip: at my destination airport, I got a luggage cart and was walking along minding my own business when a man came up beside me. He looked me in the face, so I stopped and turned. He looked me square in the eye.

"Do I know you?" he asked with a gross, insinuating look.

"No!" I said loudly, totally out of patience and disgusted by the whole thing. "I don't know you, and you don't know me." I stormed off.

Some sins are much easier to hate than others, but, gentlemen, we must hate all sin more and more every day, or we'll never make it through the enemy's premeditated attacks on our marriages, families, character, ministries, and reputations.

Hate sin!

Hate Your Life

Jesus went even further than that and said we must hate our own lives. That doesn't mean we dislike or treat ourselves badly. It means we readily give our lives, at His command, for anyone and everyone around us. We don't live to satisfy ourselves but to serve God and others.

My older brother is a great example. He was a multimillionaire and built an apocalypse-ready compound to keep his family safe should society turn chaotic. "I'm ready for the zombies, man," he would tell me, laughing. He had underground rooms, metal shutters that closed with the touch of a button, guns that could destroy an engine block from a mile away.

He died instantly when another car T-boned his. None of that stuff could protect him from the day the Lord called him home, and that is true for each of us. God commissions us to make the most of every day for His purposes, and to count our lives lost for the sake of knowing Jesus Christ. He bought us with a price: His own blood. We don't own ourselves anymore. That's what "hating our lives" means—His will, not ours.

Just how dangerous are you? It depends on how much you love your own life. Revelation 12 tells us that real overcomers "loved not their lives even unto death." They remind me of the men, many of them teenagers, who have volunteered to fight in America's past wars. They surrendered their lives to defend freedom and American principles. These days, technology and money have allowed us to outsource a lot of warring, but something in a man's character is lost when we do that. Today's "warriors" may never even see a battlefield. They kill guys with a joystick, then go home to their suburban mini mansions. Their lives are never on the line. The point is, too many guys still love their lives.

Dangerous gentlemen daily reckon themselves dead to selfishness, sin, and temptation. That's the price we pay to be great.

Love Mercy

While hating our own lives, we must love the things God loves. Chief among them is mercy.

I saw the power of this in Tunisia on an unusual mission that started with a short film our ministry made, based on a true story. A young man appeared in it whose father lived in Tunisia. This father was so moved by the film that he kept begging to meet us.

"Please, come to Tunisia," he would say. "I would love to meet you in person."

He was rich and very powerful, but Tunisia was a hotbed of recruitment for ISIS, which meant we needed a really good reason to go there. Buddy checked the father out; he seemed pretty clean. Rumor had it he was running to be president. But rather than go to Tunisia, we agreed to meet the man in France.

Eileen, Buddy, and I were on our way there when he called. "I'm so sorry. I can't leave Tunisia now because of meetings," he said. "Can you come visit me here, at my home?"

Another gut check.

Lord, what should we do? Will it be safe to go? we prayed.

We all felt good about it, so we agreed to hop a quick flight and spend a day and a night in Tunisia at the man's desert compound. A car was waiting to pick us up when we landed, and handlers escorted us through the airport, past other lines.

At the curb, Buddy did his typical thing. "Stand by the car and I'll take a photo of you and Eileen," he said. What he was really doing was sending the license plate number to our people to check out.

The short drive we expected turned out to be an hour and a half, which is a very long time in a foreign country where you don't know anybody. We left the city and traveled along a route snaking between mountains and the Mediterranean Sea. The sunset was beautiful, but the longer the ride became, the more we wondered if we were being kidnapped.

Then our driver turned off the main road. It was dark. We all looked at each other. There were no streetlights, and the road was bumpy. Why would one of the wealthiest people in Tunisia live on a bumpy road? I would have expected to be picked up in a helicopter before journeying down a dark, poorly maintained backroad. Just as we were getting concerned, we saw a truck driving toward us. It slowed down and we slowed down. In the truck were guys with guns. We had to make a decision. Eileen and I felt like waiting to see what developed, but Buddy was seriously considering snapping the driver's neck and taking over the vehicle.

"How about I put my belt around his neck and pull him into the back seat so you can drive?" I suggested as a compromise.

Meanwhile, our driver was having a long conversation with the truck guys. Eventually, they said, "Follow us."

As we began moving again, the plan to take over the vehicle was still in place and ready to be implemented. The road narrowed, and then a wall appeared beside us, indicating some kind of compound. We pulled into a tiny driveway before a tunnel with huge, Renaissance-looking wooden doors in the middle of it. They opened as if on their own and we entered the most outrageous estate I could have imagined. Against a mountain wall was what appeared to be a castle—the main living area, it turned out. On the flat area were stables for the man's Arabian horses, a petting zoo with giraffes and camels, multiple homes, an elite hotel, and immaculately kept grounds with fountains, foliage, and magnificent lighting. It felt like the best of the modern and ancient worlds merged together. Guarding it were a pack of German shepherds staked out on chains, ready to be released and turned into man-mangling weapons should anyone foolishly try to transgress.

Skipping most of the details, that night we held a screening of my short film that the man's son appeared in; he wept. Afterward, we enjoyed a massive Mediterranean dinner, probably never to be equaled in my life.

Then the man asked, "Victor, would you allow us to interview you for one of my TV networks?"

"Where?" I asked.

"In the capital," he said.

"No, sir. I don't leave your compound," I told him.

"Okay. I'll have them bring a crew out tomorrow morning," he said. "I have a special friend who can interview you."

That was that. Eileen and I slept in a wing of the hotel, two or three stories high; it felt like something from an exotic movie with satin curtains blowing in a perfect breeze, a huge bathroom, and ornate but not ostentatious decor.

The next morning, the "special friend" arrived to interview me. I didn't recognize him, but Buddy's eyes got as big as saucers. This man apparently was the personal cleric for Muammar Gaddafi, and had traveled from Libya to interview me for the show.

The first thing he asked when the cameras got rolling was, "Do you work for the CIA?"

Thank God the answer was no, because if I were CIA, they literally might have driven me to another location in Tunisia to enjoy the scenery and a nice walk back.

Then he asked, "Do you support your current administration and president?"

"No, I don't," I said truthfully. He was happy to hear that.

Then he queried me about the same topics most people want to hear about: how I learned to disarm people so fast, my turbulent childhood, and how I became a Christian.

Afterward, we had lunch. "I have one question," the cleric said, as if he had been mulling it over since our interview. "How could you forgive your stepfather for what he did to you?"

It was another opportunity to share about the power of Christ for those who believe, including the incredible power to forgive. Muslims have a hard time understanding Christian forgiveness. It is not part of their religion like it is ours, so this man was more than intrigued; he seemed deeply moved. At that moment, I realized the entire trip may have happened for the sake of that specific conversation. This influential cleric heard firsthand how the Gospel empowers us to forgive even our worst enemies and tormentors.

"Would you please come to Libya?" he asked as we parted. "Our country needs help, and Tunisia doesn't have a chance if Libya is not stable."

I told him we would consider it and pray for the opportunity. That pleased him. We left the compound with several new friends.

But what if I hadn't forgiven my father and stepfather? What then? I couldn't have taken that message to those individuals. A fast disarm impresses people but doesn't change hearts. It only opens doors. But now I had friends who wanted to continue the conversation about spiritual things.

The truth is, I'm just a kid from Louisiana who nobody wanted, who grew up to meet Jesus and forgive people who did really bad things to him. But that's all you need to change the world. God really does choose the powerless and unlikely to participate in His assignments. This promise isn't just for me; it's for you. Every dangerous gentleman must love mercy as God loves it. When we do, He shines through our choices and our lives with a power greater than wealth or weapons.

Hate the Pedestal

Stories like that have a downside: they make people think my life is way more exotic and adventurous than it is. Nobody, including me, lives in a constant, real-time action movie, but I'm here to caution you that whenever others elevate you for doing what dangerous gentlemen do—being brave, standing strong, protecting the weak, etc.—you will be in danger of getting puffed up. This can happen in a small group of five people or on the international stage before millions. Human nature is so corrupt it will take any evidence of one's alleged superiority and launch it into full-blown pride.

Pride is more dangerous than any physical weapon. It can kill the soul. We must learn to hate being on the pedestal. Otherwise, it will destroy us.

Personally, I am really bothered by Christians' tendency to treat each other like rock stars. People who are more public are not any more special or talented than those who are not. To treat each other as celebrities is really against God's heart.

When people start elevating me, I tell them honestly, "I've done cowboying, but I'm no cowboy. I worked on a ranch and rode a horse, but I would never say I'm a full-blown rancher. I've been in combat and had to make some decisions, and people definitely died because of it, but I wouldn't call myself a professional war fighter." All of that is true. I am a minister called to work in violent places, at times actively defending my own life and others', but I am in no sense an elite warrior.

The truth is, my story would be much less effective if I were a professional warrior, because that level is unattainable to most. My job really is to give others a vision for what normal people (like me) must become in the future. We have to quit being passive, believing others will protect us, our children, our communities, and our churches. We need more backbone, more fight, more resistance to evil. In the very near future, there will be thousands of people like me around the world. God is taking ordinary people—ordinary men, especially—and calling us to do extraordinary things in our generation.

Let me say this clearly: no Christian is better than another Christian based on an assignment. My assignments in Iraq and elsewhere are no more important than me or anyone else being home and raising godly kids. Neither are yours. What matters is faithfulness to what we are called to do—and trust me, doing assignments in the public eye is a lot harder than doing them when nobody knew me except the kids in youth prisons.

God gives each of us exciting things to do, but my only true excitement in life is my relationship with Him. He never disappoints me. When I go to bed, I say, "Lord, did I follow You today? I know I talked a lot of talk, but did I follow You today?" His answer is what matters.

Whenever you find yourself elevated and receiving a lot of attention and praise, leap off that pedestal and land back at His feet, where you belong.

CHAPTER 12

A DANGEROUS GENERATION

When dangerous gentlemen and their wives raise dangerous kids, we create a dangerous generation. That's one reason Eileen and I started taking our kids to Iraq. But they did not exactly erupt with joy when we invited them to join us.

"Why?" a couple of them asked.

"Because we want to do this ministry as a family," I said.

"It's hot in Iraq," another said.

"Yes, it is," I said. Unlike the Eubank kids, ours were not raised in the jungle and had a greater appreciation for things like air-conditioning.

They looked at each other to gauge their collective resistance, but after a little more discussion, they got on board and even a little excited. We started training them in first aid, situational awareness, and what it's like to ride in an armored vehicle where the windows don't roll down and the AC is out. I taught them how to put on body armor and a helmet, and how to load an AK-47 and actually shoot one. I taught them how to jump from one rooftop to another if things got weird and we had to run. I didn't expect any of that to happen, but that's the point—you never know.

A couple of weeks before our departure, our eleven-year-old son, whom we call the man-cub, asked, "Dad, can I talk to you?"

"Sure, what's up?" I said.

"Are you going to put us anywhere where ISIS can get us?"

This kid has always been a thinker and a very direct communicator, like his mom. He also wanted things to be real, like his old man. For instance, when he was five, he took classes at our karate school but told us he didn't like doing karate because he had to hit with control.

"I want to hit as hard as I can and get hit as hard as they can," he said. Real.

In response to his question about ISIS, I asked him a question in return.

"Have you been thinking about this?"

"Yessir."

"You worried?" I asked.

"Yessir."

"That's normal," I reassured him. "You're an eleven-year-old going to a war zone in Iraq. You've heard about what happens there. What you're feeling is normal—but it's not right. Here's the reason."

He looked at me, waiting.

"Right now, we're at our house in the US, with a fence, guns, dogs, and stuff," I said. "Are you in any danger right now?"

"No, sir," he said.

"But you're having the mental and physical responses as if you were in danger," I said. "It's a waste of your energy, son. It's called worry. It's like a rocking chair. It gives you something to do but it gets you nowhere. Put that energy, instead, into assessing and planning. Don't start living fearfully. Fear will rob you of your faith and debilitate you."

He nodded. It made sense to him.

"To answer your actual question, Mom and Dad will never put you in a place where ISIS can get you," I said. "We won't take you into Mosul. You'll stay in the safe house. But the reality is, it's Iraq. It's war. You're only a short drive from where ISIS is. But for them to specifically come get us, there's a lot of redundancy of security: checkpoints, walls, soldiers, our team, your mom, me."

He nodded again.

"And I'll assure you of this," I continued. "If something happens, you'll be the first to know. I won't hide it from you if we're in potential danger. But guess what? You're trained. And you'll get more training over there."

"Alright, Dad," he said.

"Feel better?"

"Yeah," he said, and went off happily.

Of course, Eileen and I hadn't lightly decided to take our kids into a war zone, especially since by then it was more widely known who we were and what we were doing there. Our own head of security had told us, "You have to start sharing what you're doing on social media."

"Why?" I asked. "I don't want ISIS to know we're here."

He leaned back and roared with laughter.

"Brother, they already know who you are," he said. "They hate you. So you must get millions of Muslims to love you for how you are helping their people. That will be part of your security."

So we reversed strategy and went from covert to overt. Iraqis kept asking, "How can you bring your kids to this place?" By then, we could honestly say, "Our children are part of this assignment, and they are not any more valuable than your children." That surprised them, but for us it was a reality. We weren't going leave them out of the massive thing God was doing because of fear or because we thought they were more special than the war orphans we cared for. No way.

That said, I'm still a dad and do everything in my power to protect my family. We traveled with Scout and both our American and in-country security teams. We did everything we knew to do to stay safe in that environment.

There was one last aspect of that. When we arrived, I went to Hassan, my primary security guy in Iraq. I had to have a super-direct conversation with him about the new circumstances. By then, he had partnered with us for a few years. He was a legend in the intel community for doing behind-the-scenes work, including killing several bad guys in critical situations. Delta trained him and trusted him, and I'd been with him at a FOB where special ops guys he'd worked with tried their hardest to recruit him back, including with the lure of big paychecks. Hassan made me proud: "No, thank you," he said. "I only want to work for Victor Marcus now." It wasn't about money anymore. It was about, "if I die, it will be in service of this cause, not that one."

But now that I was bringing my kids into Iraq, I needed to be certain of his level of commitment.

"Hassan, I need to ask you something," I said.

"Yes?"

I got close to him to watch his pupils and the pulse on his neck. I was looking for any change in his physiology or demeanor.

"Hassan, my family is here," I said. "I know you have three daughters. If ISIS finds out you're working with me and they kidnap one of your daughters to try to force you to turn us over to them, are you going to roll on us?"

I watched for any sign, any flinch, any tightening of the pupils, any acceleration of the neck pulse. What happened next caught me off guard. His eyes got watery, and tears began seeping out of the sides.

He's already turned on us! I thought, going worst-case scenario in my mind. But before I could say anything, he spoke.

"You are my big brother," he said. "I only have one. I am young enough to have more children, but I can never have another one of you."

That kind of loyalty is pure Arab warrior culture and is unknown in most parts of the world. It's no wonder my kids call Hassan "uncle," and his children call me "grandfather." Hassan is family.

A Dangerous Rescue

That summer proved to be really meaningful—and safe—for our family as we hosted and helped kids at the house and did an assortment of other cool things. The kids worked their butts off, going with us into IDP camps, handing out lions and lambs, and helping us comfort rescued children. One day we got a call from a general saying his troops had pulled a little girl out of a pile of concrete rubble. Her parents had been killed. Did we want to help find her relatives or a new home for her? We said yes and immediately traveled through innumerable checkpoints to Mosul to pick her up.

The precious little girl—black hair, chubby cheeks, and innocent, haunting black eyes—was probably fifteen or sixteen months old. She had lice in her hair, was malnourished and dehydrated, and seemed injured. We put her in our vehicle and prepared to hide her at each checkpoint. If she was seen, we would have to bribe the security guys to get her through.

I remember that rescue distinctly because at one checkpoint, the man in charge wouldn't let us through. As Americans, we never wanted to stay at checkpoints for long because that was exactly where we might get attacked. Someone would call their ISIS cousin, and bad guys would come to get the party started.

The longer we sat there, the more furious I became. I was definitely in protective mode with that little girl in Eileen's arms. Our paperwork was correct, but that arrogant little commander was flexing his control or wanting money or something. We couldn't figure it out, but eventually I lost my composure and began yelling at him.

"I want your name and where you live!" I shouted, implying that I would come after him. It was the only time I ever got so angry that my team had to intervene.

"Hey, boss, it's okay," Hassan said, and helped pull me back from the dark side, where you start to do things you regret.

Finally, we called a major decision-maker in that area, who called the little local checkpoint guy directly and said, "My assistant told you to let them through and you didn't. I will kill you and your family if they're not let through immediately."

At that point, I saw something I had never seen before: The Iraqi checkpoint boss turned green with fear. Literally, he became green. We grabbed our passports from his hands, walked out, and got home safely with the tiny prize from the battlefield in our arms.

I was wrung out from the day and especially glad that our kids were there to help the girl acclimate to her new situation.

"Hey," I said to one of my daughters when we walked in. "Nobody knows this little girl's name. Her parents were killed, and she has no known family. Give her a name and check her for lice. She keeps scratching her head."

"Alright," she said, and started playing with the baby—holding her, cleaning her up, and feeding her. The little girl didn't know how to drink out of a baby bottle, so we had to mix formula in a water bottle and let her drink it from there.

Little kids prefer to be with other kids, even older ones, so having our children there created instant rapport. The next morning, I went into the living area and found her cleaned up from the grime of war, wearing a little dress, toddling around, and playing with the dog. Our kids had washed her hair and put it in ponytails that pointed straight up. Because she reminded them of a little girl in the movie *Monsters, Inc.,* they named her Boo.

After several days, her relatives were located, and Boo went to live with them. She was one of many precious ones who passed through our home.

A Grenade for His Birthday

There were plenty of ups and downs that summer. Each of us got sick at one time or another, which is common in Iraq. It's hard to describe an atmosphere that has so much death in it. When dust storms kick up, all the junk on the ground flies around and gets on you and in you. We woke up some mornings with a layer of fine sand on our faces, our sheets, and every other surface in the house. To make it worse, in July and August in Iraq, the very bowels of the earth open up and vent their heat.

One day I went into the bathroom to find my eleven-year-old son lying in the shower in a fetal position with cold water running over his body. That was common. We all did that to alleviate the misery of being sick in triple-digit weather.

Eileen and I both found ourselves really ill on the man-cub's birthday. We lay in bed with fevers, too weak to get up. Chaz and the team got him some type of cupcake and put a candle in it. We missed the celebration, but the next morning, when I was strong enough to pull myself downstairs, my son shot straight with me, as usual.

"Dad, worst birthday ever," he announced.

"I believe you," I said. "Stuck in the Middle East in hundred-degree weather, with no gifts and no adequate celebration. That's about as bad as it gets."

Then a thought hit me.

"Hey, do you want to hold a grenade for your birthday?" I asked. He was turning twelve; it seemed appropriate.

"Yeah!" he replied.

I unbuttoned a grenade pouch on my kit and took out a live one. He watched with great interest, his face brightening, eyes riveted on the explosive device. We stepped outside with it, just to be safe.

"Alright, hold out your hands," I said. He did and I set the weapon into his palms. He beamed, looking it over intently.

"Can I pull the pin?" he asked after a moment.

"No," I said, thinking, *This is not really the right place to do that, in a neighborhood and all. You'd need to be behind a concrete wall somewhere, then throw it, duck, and plug your ears.*

But I didn't need to explain all that. He nodded and we both laughed, loving everything about this moment. I glanced over my shoulder, a little worried about what Eileen would think if she saw us handling the explosive. But I also felt a sense of redemption.

"Tell me another twelve-year-old who's held a live grenade in Iraq," I said to him proudly.

"You're right," he said—which was a compliment coming from him.

"This memory will only get cooler as you get older," I promised him. A little while later, I put the grenade back in its pouch. I could tell my son was satisfied with how his birthday had turned out.

On another occasion, we were all together in an IDP camp when the man-cub came up to me.

"Dad, see those kids over there?" he said.

"Yeah?"

"They keep trying to get me to walk around the side of the building."

"Why?" I asked.

"One kid wants to fight me," he said. "What do I do?"

"Number one, don't walk around that corner," I said. A big rule in combat zones is not to go off with locals by yourself, because you can get hurt. They'll shoot you and blame ISIS. There were certainly children of ISIS in that camp, and probably in that group of boys.

"But," I continued, "if he wants to fight, don't back down. If he touches you, rip into him."

My son nodded. I'm sorry for anyone who feels like fighting is never an option. I tell my kids that fighting is the last thing you want to do, but you have to know how to do it and be willing to do it, if the situation calls for it.

"Okay," he said and went off to rejoin the kids.

I sort of forgot about the situation until he came back half an hour later—in the company of the kid who had wanted to fight him. They were both acting jovial.

"What's going on?" I asked.

"I let him know, 'If you want to fight, alright; let's go,'" my son said. "Then he didn't want to fight."

Without knowing it, he had pulled a total dangerous gentleman move. The kids there just wanted to know he wasn't some cowardly American, and he proved it.

Escape from Iraq

Three days before our scheduled flight home, the FBI contacted our team.

"Are you with Victor Marx?" the man on the phone said. "We are hearing chatter that ISIS would very much like to get him."

That was the only time I felt gripping fear during a Middle East assignment. The thought of my family paying a price for our work in Iraq was more than I could bear.

Our team went on instant high alert. When ISIS wants to kill you, they will sacrifice any number of foot soldiers to do it. For example, if you're in a guarded compound, they'll pull up in a van. One guy jumps out, the van moves away, and then the guy walks up to the front gate and blows up himself and everyone in the vicinity. Then another guy gets out of the van, runs into the courtyard, and detonates his explosive vest, too, killing the guards. A third guy then runs to the doors of the building and clacks off another vest, *boom*! A fourth runs down the hall and detonates his vest, killing the interior security guards. A fifth runs to the doors of the locked room you're in and blows them open, killing himself. Then a sixth guy runs into your room, clacks off his vest, and kills you. That's the level of commitment they come at you with.

A thousand questions filled our minds: *Was our safe house compromised? Were the guards at the gate susceptible to bribes? How many guys with guns outside and inside would we need to really defend ourselves? What if ISIS staked out a road near our gated community and got us coming or going? What would they do with our kids if they captured them?*

The guy in charge of our response was Sam, a globally recognized specialist who served, then and now, as my international head of security. One American magazine labeled him the most wanted man by terrorists around the world. Sam is a top-level hunter of bad guys. ISIS had tried to kill him eight times. Delta used him for its operations. He was part of the team that killed al Qaeda leader Ayman al-Zawahiri. In fact, when the operators who killed him rifled through his pockets, they found a paper with Sam's license plate number on it. That's how much Sam got inside people's heads.

Now Sam was going to keep us alive, because if anybody knew how to outwit and outrun bad guys, it was him. "We have to get you out of the country in thirty-six hours," he said, and I could hear the anger and urgency in his voice. "Don't tell anyone, but get your family and go to this location."

We did exactly that. After a bit, he called again.

"Time to move," he said. "Get to this next location."

We again obeyed, but even moving around was dangerous. ISIS functions like all cartels and gangs do, keeping scouts on every corner, in every city, looking for armored vehicles and things, making calls, texting: "Americans heading north." Iraq also had lots of checkpoints where you had to pull out your passport and state your business. You never knew whose cousin worked there, and which one might take a picture and send it to ISIS to get a $500 finder's fee. That was how things worked in that country.

Sam called one last time that night.

"Your flights are now set at ten in the morning," he said. "Get there eight hours before the flight."

That meant leaving at midnight because if ISIS were setting up a hit, they would be waiting for us on the road to the airport unless we got past first. So we caught a few hours of uneasy sleep—at least Eileen and the kids did—and in the wee hours of the morning, our team made it safely to the airport.

But when we went to the counter of the major Middle Eastern airline we were flying on, three of our tickets had been canceled: Eileen's, mine, and our son's.

"Why?" our security guy demanded.

"Sir, I don't know," the man at the counter said. "It says the flight is sold out."

"It wasn't sold out when we bought tickets," our guy said.

I pulled out my wallet. "Give me three more tickets," I said, and handed the airline guy a credit card. He looked at it and shook his head.

"We cannot take your credit card," he said.

"Why?" we demanded again. He shook his head and gave no answer.

It was looking to us like outside interference, and I was getting ready to climb over the counter and throttle Mr. Airline Representative. We knew insiders at the airline were sometimes paid by ISIS to track someone; we'd seen it before. Some invisible actor would check every flight manifest, find anyone with the target's last name, and cancel his tickets. But we also had learned that the only way to counter ISIS was with the tools ISIS itself used to control people: money and fear.

Fear was already working as the airline guy saw the intensity in my eyes. He developed that sheen of perspiration and that frequent gulping pattern you want to see in your opponent at times like that. I pulled out a substantial amount of cash and said calmly but with a hint of insanity: "You're going to get me tickets on this flight. I don't care if it's first class, business class, or what. Get us seats, now."

I set the money down. The man's eyes flicked from the pile of cash to the computer screen, and he began typing wildly. Within minutes, to his great relief, we had new tickets, and they worked. The flight wasn't "sold out" after all. We boarded the plane and flew home. The ISIS chatter came to nothing.

We debriefed about the trip as a family when we got home, but it was a whole year later when my son came up to me with something to say.

"Hey, Dad, remember how I asked you if we would be in danger in Iraq, and you asked if I was afraid?" he said.

"I sure do," I said.

"When it really happened and we had to hide and all that, I never felt afraid," he said. "Not once."

My buttons were bursting.

"God gave you the grace for courage," I said.

He nodded as if this were perfectly normal, then went back to what he was doing. That's when I knew for sure that we were raising dangerous kids.

The Bully

That mettle was tested when the man-cub faced a challenge on the home front from a would-be tough kid—but this episode ended up being more serious.

The summer after we took our kids to Iraq, I invited a retired Special Forces operator, whose marriage had fallen apart, to live on-site and help us build our training center. At my invitation, he brought his teenage son—a big, older kid who was thoroughly rebellious. As the pair went about their tasks, that kid mouthed off loudly to his dad and then to others. His impertinence grew worse by the day.

"I was deployed his whole life," his dad told me by way of an apology. "I was out killing bad guys. I wasn't there to raise him."

Clearly. That kid was angry and violent, and I knew from my experience ministering in youth prisons that unless there was some course correction, he'd wind up in one. He had even punched his sister and his mom while his dad was away. A summer working together was supposed to help heal his relationship with his dad, but so far that kid was exhibiting none of the hoped-for change. For my part, I tried to see him from the best possible perspective, as a future leader like his dad, who was a heroic leader in the special operations community. But some days it was hard to hold onto that hopeful view.

Eventually, the kid started mouthing off to our man-cub, right on our property. This badgering went on day after day. Finally, the Future Leader said something derogatory about Eileen to another kid.

"What did you say?!?" my son asked.

"Oh, nothing, nothing," the kid said, then blamed the other kid for saying it.

The man-cub flushed and came to join me in the house.

"Dad, can I fight this kid?" he asked. "This has been going on for too long."

Everyone on the property knew the boy had created an atmosphere of conflict, and that things had to come to a head somehow. It looked like it was up to the man-cub to bring them back to normal.

"If you're fighting for the right thing, yeah," I said.

"Okay," he said.

The next day, Future Leader disrespected me—and that was the last straw for the man-cub. My son walked up to him and jumped on him. They began to scrap it up pretty good in the dirt, but soon the kid overpowered him and pinned him to the ground. He exulted loudly, "I whooped you!"

My boy shoved him off, got up, and squared himself to take him on again. They laid into each other, not throwing punches to the face, but grappling and wrestling. A second time, Future Leader took him to the ground and pinned him. He was bigger and older, and it was clear he had been fighting like this for much of his life.

"I whooped you!" he shouted again.

I was over in the house, where team members gather, when the man-cub stormed in, his clothes disheveled, dirt in his hair, and fuming. He stomped into a back room. I followed him.

"Son, how did it go?" I asked gently.

"Not good at all," he said. "I couldn't beat him!"

He was so emotional that he was tearing up. It meant a lot to him to be able to defend his parents against the boy's insults.

"Well," I said, chiding him a bit, "you should have been training."

My son had recently stopped training in jiu-jitsu and karate, and it was showing in the outcome of his skirmish.

"I hate to point it out, but even if you're in the right, if your physical skills aren't developed and honed, you won't have victory," I continued.

"I know!" he shouted angrily, because he regretted not being ready for the moment.

Then one of those phrases jumped into my mind that I knew must be from the Holy Spirit.

"Let me ask you something," I said. "He whooped you, but did he win?"

"What?" the man-cub said.

"I know he beat you, but did he win?" I asked again.

"What do you mean?" he asked.

"You're fighting for what's right," I said. "Have you changed your mind about what that is, or do you still believe that he is wrong?"

"He's wrong," he said firmly.

"So he didn't change your mind about it?" I asked.

"No, sir," he said.

"Okay, so …?" I asked.

"He didn't win. He just whooped me," the man-cub agreed, a smile breaking through the tears. Life was coming back into him.

Then he looked up at me. "Can I fight him again?" he asked.

I thought a moment. "Of course," I said.

Just as we said this, Future Leader burst into the house. He stood in the middle of the living area and crowed, "I beat him! I beat him!" I knew his dad must be thinking, *You just beat the fire out of Victor's son. He's my boss. What is wrong with you?*

The man-cub looked at me as if to say, "I have a green light, right?"

I nodded and said, "Go get you some."

He tore out of the room, down the hall, into the living room, and hit that kid full stride, body on body. The Future Leader freaked out from the surprise, and they began fighting like hyenas, throwing each other around the room. I came out of the room where I'd been, and the dad came over to me and asked, "Should we stop them and bring them into the dojo to fight?"

"No, let them settle it once and for all right here," I said.

As the boys scrapped, we moved chairs and tables to give them room. It was a good, fair fight, but in the end, my friend's son took my boy to the ground again and pinned him. Thinking he had proved every point there was to prove, he stood up and released my son, who promptly tackled him again. In an instant they were back on the floor thrashing around. Yet again, the kid pinned my boy.

"I beat you!" he said, but this time added, "Now, stop!"

The man-cub leapt to his feet, unbowed, and came after him again. Then the unexpected happened: Future Leader walked over to the stairs, sat down, put his hands on his face, and started crying. It wasn't wimpy crying. It was mature pain coming out. The adults in the room all looked at each other in disbelief.

"I don't even like to fight!" the kid shouted. "Why won't he stop?"

His will had been broken. My son's determination had pushed him beyond his limits. In fighting terms, the kid had tapped out.

"Why won't he stop?" he kept saying between sobs. "Why won't he stop?"

I spoke up: "Number one, he's a Marx. It's in his DNA. Second, he's fighting for what's right. You're fighting for what's wrong."

As I spoke, I was holding the man-cub back because he smelled victory. Having broken the kid's spirit, he wanted to finally whoop him physically. But the time for fighting was over.

"Hey, let's go get some Hawaiian food," Chaz intervened, and escorted my son out of the house. Meanwhile, the kid's dad stood next to his son, saying, "What is wrong with you? When are you going to learn? I *wanted* his son to whoop you!"

It wasn't the way I would have done it, or the words I would have used, but I left them alone to work it out.

A few hours later, the man-cub and Chaz came back. I caught the boy before he went outside.

"Just make sure you watch your back, because I don't know where that kid is or what he's thinking," I warned him.

He nodded and went out. Sure enough, Future Leader saw him and approached, but this time, without anger or threat.

"I'm sorry," he said. "And I'm an" (he used a term I won't repeat). Those within hearing distance were stunned by his words. It was the first moment of humility any one of us had seen from him.

"Can we just be friends?" the kid asked.

The man-cub didn't even hesitate.

"Yeah, just stop treating people so disrespectfully," he said, "and don't talk about my mom that way."

Future Leader nodded. The conflict ended then and there. Even better, that kid quit making everyone miserable with his disrespectful mouth.

Dangerous kids and adults know what it means to fight for what's right. I'm all for avoiding physical fights whenever possible, but these things usually aren't physical. More often they come in other venues, in other ways: in a classroom or in front of a school board. At a church that's going woke, or at a city council meeting. The possibilities are endless. Regardless of the form it takes, the inner will to win that my son exhibited is exactly what we all must have as parents, citizens, and leaders.

My boy proved to me again that day that when we're fighting for the right thing, we never lose if we never give up. That's exactly what God wants us to instill in the kids He gives us to raise.

CONCLUSION

I wish I had more time and more pages.

We have so many stories of many women and children who have been helped in extreme ways, some of which can never be shared. I have so many examples of dangerous gentlemen working around the world—unnoticed and uncelebrated, but champions in the eyes of Heaven. I have so many stories of times when the angels of God surely protected us beyond what we know. And still, I know there is much more ahead for us—and for you.

Whatever God has done through our ministry is a glimpse of what He wants for the church of the future—and I am convinced every believer is called to be part of it. It is time for dangerous gentlemen to stand tall and lay down our lives for the weak and vulnerable. It's time for greater risk-taking, more compassion, more power, and deeper self-sacrifice in the church. It's time for men to once again boldly protect our communities from physical threats, moral filth, and predators. It's time for the fathers and mature men of this nation to proclaim righteousness, love the needy, and bring justice back into fashion.

Eileen and I are living proof that whoever you are, you can transform lives and circumstances around you with boldness, fearlessness, and the gentle heart of God. That doesn't require going overseas. It requires saying yes to the specific assignment God has tailored especially for you, then never letting go. If weak and busted people like us can do it, you can, too. Each one of us is powerful and purposeful in Christ. We all are invited to lead adventurous lives in Him.

God Will Do What You Can't

When I feel a task or a challenge is beyond me, I often remind myself of situations in which God has saved my bacon when there was little I could do.

I remember doing a recon mission of a Burmese-controlled army unit and seeing Russian assets in there with them—really bad news for anyone opposing them. Our little team was huddled in the jungle, peering at the military compound from a hidden position, knowing these were some of the worst people on the planet. Burmese army soldiers burn villages for sport, loot whatever they want, and rape the women and girls. They have even killed missionary girls. Their evil is just as boundless as that of ISIS. Our objective was to observe, record, and develop a report to send to the United Nations and any media we could reach about the atrocities this army was committing.

Suddenly, the gates of the compound opened, and a team of Burmese soldiers came marching up the hill in our direction. Dave and I looked at each other, having no idea if the soldiers knew we were there, but knowing there was only one path through the area—and we were on it. If we fled, there was every possibility they would hear us and pursue. Being severely outmanned, we didn't want any kind of confrontation, but if they came up the trail, we would have to engage them somehow. All we had were semi-automatic rifles, and not the fancy kind. They were the kind that made you pray, "Oh, Lord, please let this thing work." Our ammunition was limited.

If they found us, they would either fire on us or take us prisoner, and then we'd be in for some rough treatment and maybe an urgent diplomatic situation.

I heard the sound of their boots against the dry jungle soil, drawing nearer. Before we could try to sneak away, a profoundly loud noise erupted from the direction of the compound.

Kabooooom!

We hit the deck. Stuff was flying in the air. A cloud of dirt rose into the sky as bits of things began raining back down. We knew instantly what had happened: The column of soldiers had walked over one of their own landmines.

The team and I just looked at each other and laughed. What else could we do? It was divine protection, and we had seen it at work many times. We had come to rely on it. In fact, when guys didn't believe in divine protection, they got fearful and stupid.

Fearful and stupid describes one guy who was going to fly over to Iraq with us to do humanitarian operations in sketchy territory. He was a combat veteran with a lot of experience, but sitting in the airport getting ready for our big flight over, he started to tremble. It didn't stop, and it wasn't that cold out.

"Hey, man, you okay?" I asked.

"I don't know. I don't know what's happening," he told me.

"Talk to me," I said.

"We don't have a QRF, do we?"

"No, we are the QRF," I reminded him.

"So we're really doing this all alone?" he asked.

I thought, *We went over all this before, about twenty dozen times.*

"It depends on your definition of alone," I said evenly. "We have God on our side, and warring angels, and we feel we're in God's will. But there is no government help. Nobody's coming for us in that way."

He began to get emotional.

"I don't think I can do it," he said. I literally watched him be overcome with fear and anxiety.

"Let me make a command call here," I said. "You're not going to go."

He nodded in agreement.

"But will you look at me as less?" he asked.

Yes, you wuss, I thought.

"No," I said. I should have told him the truth, but I didn't want him to get on the plane. I was mad at him. We had put all this work into preparing, and the wheels were coming off his mind before we even left American soil. As a warrior, you need more self-awareness than that.

Once you've made the choice to be a dangerous gentleman, never fear, never back down, never wuss out. Count the cost, go forward, sprint to the end.

A great picture of this happened on my last mission with Dave in Iraq. The scene was pitched battle between the Iraqis and ISIS. As the army pushed into their area, Dave and I found ourselves running toward a village that ISIS had held for three years. We were the only two Americans out there. Nobody was covering us with gunfire, and there were no tanks to hide behind. It was just a rush to this village to see what innocent people we could rescue.

I was hustling across the open ground when I looked over at Dave. The guy is as Wild West as they come. He loves flinging himself into situations like that. I am typically more methodical—but this was all about raw speed and hoping the bad guys missed. Part of me wanted to laugh. Dave had knee braces on and was running stiff-legged due to injuries he has sustained from doing what he does. I liked to poke fun at him sometimes, but now I realized he was actually running faster than me.

The thought ran through my mind, *What are we doing out here? We could get killed, and then our wives are widows, and our kids and family will have to deal with it.*

Just as quickly the answer came back: *We're here because we're doing God's work and God called us to be in this place, right now. He will always lead, guide, and protect.*

With that, my competitiveness kicked in and I pushed into overdrive, running to catch Dave and maybe even pass him, if I could keep from laughing at the sheer sight and exhilaration of it all. I had no idea what would happen in the next second, the next minute, or the rest of the day, but I was certain of the call and protection of God—and with His help, I was determined to sprint to the end.

AFTERWORD

The very first step to becoming a dangerous gentleman is to surrender your life to God.

I did this when I was serving as a Marine at Camp Pendleton. Everything changed when I met Jesus. From that day on, my life has had a purpose and peace I had never experienced before. It was amazing and totally transforming.

You see, I was a messed up young man. My life was going nowhere. I badly needed direction and a reason to live. I especially wanted the affirmation of a father and a solid foundation of beliefs and principles to stand on. God met me in the middle of my massive problems. I still had a lot of work to do to get well—and I am very much still a work in progress to this day—but I have walked with Jesus the whole way, and that has made all the difference. Without Him, I am 100 percent sure I would already be dead.

I believe every person needs Jesus as much as I do. Sin separates us from God and will lead you to Hell. If you are wondering what you've done wrong, look at the Ten Commandments in the Bible, like I did as a young man. They make it clear what separates us from God. I've broken all of the commandments; you've probably broken most of them. God's rules are His mercy because they let us know we are sinful. There is nothing any of us can do to save ourselves, no matter how good our lives may seem. We all fall short somehow. We need forgiveness. We need the love of a perfect Father—but that has been made available to us through the perfect sacrifice of His only Son.

It starts with the greatest Man of all, Jesus Christ, and what He did on the cross. I hear people say, "But you don't know what I've done." I hate that phrase. You and I don't get to sit here and pick and choose what is too hard for God to forgive. The cross is either good enough for it all, or none at all. Don't limit Jesus's work through a lack of faith. Believe His forgiveness covers all your sins, because it does.

My appeal to you is simple: Respond. Surrender. Don't do it halfway. Go for it all. Don't just get saved; live for God. Be all-in. Once you're in, give it everything you have. The most miserable people I know are Christians who straddle the fence, with one foot in the world and the other in Christianity. (I straddled a metal fence one time, one foot on one side and one foot on the other. Then I slipped and fell on the twisted metal, and I'm telling you, it hurt.) What I'm saying is, choose your side and go all the way. It will help you do things you never thought possible before. In my case, when I met the Lord, I was able to forgive the stepfather who had tortured me. The forgiveness I offered was based on the forgiveness I received from God Almighty for my sin. Because of His life-long grace, I have the peace of God wherever I go and in whatever circumstance I find myself.

One of my favorite presentations of the Gospel message is Billy Graham's "Steps to Peace with God." It reads:

1. God's Plan—Peace and Life

God loves you and wants you to experience His peace and life.

The BIBLE says: "For God so loved the world that He gave His only begotten Son, that whoever believes in Him should not perish but have everlasting life" (John 3:16).

2. Our Problem—Separation

> Being at peace with God is not automatic, because by
> nature you are separated from God.

> The BIBLE says: "For all have sinned and fall short of
> the glory of God" (Romans 3:23).

3. God's Remedy—The Cross

> God's love bridges the gap of separation between God
> and you. When Jesus Christ died on the cross and rose
> from the grave, He paid the penalty for your sins.

> The BIBLE says: "He personally carried the load of
> our sins in his own body when he died on the cross"
> (1 Peter 2:24 TLB).

4. Our Response—Receive Christ

> You cross the bridge into God's family when you receive
> Christ by personal invitation.

> The BIBLE says: "But as many as received Him, to
> them He gave the right to become children of God,
> even to those who believe in His name" (John 1:12).

To receive Christ, you need to do four things:

1. ADMIT your spiritual need. "I am a sinner."
2. REPENT and be willing to turn from your sin.

3. BELIEVE that Jesus Christ died for you on the cross.

4. RECEIVE, through prayer, Jesus Christ into your heart and life.

CHRIST says, "Behold, I stand at the door and knock. If anyone hears My voice and opens the door, I will come in" (Revelation 3:20).

The BIBLE says, "Whoever calls upon the name of the Lord will be saved" (Romans 10:13).

What to Pray:

Dear Lord Jesus, I know that I am a sinner and need Your forgiveness. I believe that You died for my sins. I want to turn from my sins. I now invite You to come into my heart and life. I want to trust and follow You as Lord and Savior. In Jesus's name, Amen.[1]

Join me in this adventure. Put your life in God's trustworthy hands, submit to His authority and plan, and He will make your life greater than you've ever dreamed—even if it means hardships and, at times, suffering for His name to be glorified.

---

1 | "Steps to Peace with God" Used with permission from the Billy Graham Evangelistic Association.